INSTINCT

DAILY READINGS

INSTINCT

DAILY READINGS

100 Insights That Will Uncover, Sharpen
and Activate Your Instincts

T.D. JAKES

New York   Boston   Nashville

Hachette Book Group USA
237 Park Avenue
New York, NY 10017

Visit our website at www.faithwords.com.

Printed in the United States of America

First Edition: October 2014
10 9 8 7 6 5 4 3 2 1

ISBN: 978-1-455-56141-4

CONTENTS

INTRODUCTION

As I began to look at this inner drive called instinct, I was surprised to realize that we all have instincts. Some of us have not activated our instincts, while others have tapped into that inner wisdom to enter into new heights.

So what is instinct? It is a combination of our observations that are synthesized through the filter of who we really are and our truest goals in life; it is the combination of the facts, data, information, and knowledge that nourishes us and gives us insight. Instinct also comes from the creativity, resilience, and resourcefulness that abide within. When we activate all of these attributes, we get an inner drive that can compel us to live fulfilling lives.

I'm pleased to share with you what I've learned from studying this amazing inner drive called instinct that God has placed inside each of us. Through the pages in this book, you will read 100 short insights based on my book *Instinct: The Power to Unleash Your Inborn Drive*, which will help you tap into your heart, gut feelings, hunches, and intuition for success in every area of your life. The readings are paired with Scripture to give you daily reminders to rediscover and reclaim your inner drive one day at a time.

In addition to the daily readings in this book, you can read *Instinct* to go more in depth and learn how to activate your God-given instincts for success. I know that a more fulfilled life awaits you as you embrace your instinct and become the person you were created to be!

T. D. Jakes

INSTINCT TO THRIVE

My son, do not let wisdom and understanding out of your sight, preserve sound judgment and discretion; they will be life for you, an ornament to grace your neck. Then you will go on your way in safety, and your foot will not stumble.
Proverbs 3:21-23, NIV

Instinct comes from our Creator. We are made in God's image, and he is the giver of good and perfect gifts (James 1:17); therefore, our instincts will reflect our Creator. Instincts bear the imprint of the divine.

So if it doesn't act or look like something God would bless or smile upon, it probably isn't instinct. It could be self-indulgent desires or compulsion, but it is not instinct. Instinct is not an uncontrollable urge; it is not self-indulgent desire; it is not arbitrary impulse or compulsion. Those inclinations are human and may resemble instinct, but they are not.

Our instincts help us meet God's intention for our lives, give us and others fulfillment, and give us dominion or reign over other creatures. While all living things have a proclivity to survive—or instincts to survive—we as humans also have instincts to thrive. We can use our instincts to live well and to live better, and to help others do the same. We are to use our God-given instincts to honor God, God's people, and God's creation. When we follow instinct and refuse to let wisdom out of sight, Scripture says we will have life—a fulfilled life. Like a fine necklace, wisdom adorns and makes everything beautiful, better, and more fulfilling.

Instinct can be seen as the little extra that makes a big difference. People who use instinct see a little more and a bit clearer than those who do not. Instinct followers allow wisdom to guide them toward better and the best, ultimately giving fulfillment.

When you use insight along with intellect, you are far more likely to succeed than people who just rely on intellect or who merely do what they are expected to do. The employee who follows the job description to a "T" does what he or she is expected to do. That's nice. But the person who exceeds expectations often uses instinct to go the extra mile, to anticipate what might need to be done, or to determine what the company actually could use to run more smoothly—that isn't on the job description. These people have followed an inner compass that tells them what cannot even be described.

As you learn to listen to your instincts not only to survive, but to thrive, dig deeply and pay attention to your inner voice, your guide. Spiritual people know that prayer can uncover much. Open your heart to God and allow your Creator to guide you. Your experience and observations and knowledge can be merged together to produce powerful insight that you and only you have. And only you can deliver it to the world. Whether in a small way or in a large way, we are all called to have an impact. You were born for a reason. Use your instincts to thrive, not simply to survive.

Prayer
Lord, I thank you for giving me instincts and creating me to not only survive, but to thrive. Help me to open my heart to you and to the deep inclinations you've placed within me.
In Jesus' name. Amen.

DISCOVER INSTINCT

Knowing what is right is like deep water in the heart; a wise person draws from the well within.
Proverbs 20:5, MSG

Many think instinct is something that only highly successful and prominent people have; they think the ordinary Joe just doesn't have it. But this couldn't be further from the truth. Instinct is very natural, and it is inside each of us.

No one is born without instincts. All of us have internal senses beyond the physical with which we can better determine what's next, what's safe, or even what's right. Our instincts speak to us daily, prompting us to pay attention, to listen more carefully, to sidestep danger, and to seize an opportunity.

Some may be more in tune with their instincts—and these people will tend to be more outwardly successful and maybe even more notable because of their accomplishments, but that doesn't mean they have anything we ourselves do not possess. Everyone has instincts, but some may be less inclined to listen to them. We, like all of God's creatures, come complete with instincts on the inside. From this inner sanctum springs wisdom we don't even know we possess. But in a fast-paced, busy world, we tend not to give ourselves the quiet moments of reflection that are needed to unleash our instincts.

Think about it: there are some things you just know. You don't even know how or why you know, you just do. This inner knowing is instinctive. It is as natural as the ability to sense when you've found the thing you were born to do. Unfortunately, many of us often spend our lives doing what we were trained to do. Some do what they were asked to do. And most of us to do what others need us to do. All the while, we wonder why the feeling of fulfillment eludes us.

Our Creator designed everything intentionally. Yet most of us live our lives wondering what God's intention for our life is. Worse still, there's an aching in our hearts as we sense that there has to be more in life: something beyond the monotonous compliance with convenient opportunities, which is the way most of us have lived our lives. It's why so many hard-working people dread going to work—not because they are lazy, but because they are unfulfilled. Those who are in touch with their instincts are like the ones described in today's Proverb; they draw out the wisdom that's in the heart. They spend time paying attention to motives as well as to what really stirs them. They don't ignore their passions or what God has placed in their hearts.

Without understanding the guidance that our innate God-given instincts provide us, we simply adjust to the urgency of circumstances, all the while sensing deep within that we were created for so much more. Yet the uncertainty or fear of pursuing this inner sense keeps us contained in the contrived cage of the ordinary. Simply put, we've never learned to rely on our instincts.

Regardless of where we are in life, it's not too late to align our lives with the inner wisdom of who we really are and what we were made to do. God, the Master Designer, has equipped us with a fundamental instinct that draws us to our divine reason for being. This sense of potential being realized is more fulfilling than any paycheck. It is the feeling of fitting in, like a piece in a puzzle, to form a greater picture than what we may be doing right now. It is the innate satisfaction that comes from giving the gifts that you and you alone can contribute to the world.

✪ ✪ ✪ ✪

Prayer
God, my Savior and Creator, please help me to pay attention to the stirrings in my heart. Help me use faith and wisdom to unlock those things you have called me to do.
In Jesus' name. Amen.

INSTINCTS AND IDENTITY

Let perseverance finish its work so that you may be mature and complete, not lacking anything. If any of you lacks wisdom, you should ask God, who gives generously to all without finding fault, and it will be given to you. But when you ask, you must believe and not doubt, because the one who doubts is like a wave of the sea, blown and tossed by the wind.

James 1:4-6, NIV

Deeply spiritual people pray for true wisdom to be revealed. They understand that following instincts is really about following what God has placed inside of each of us. Are you ready to pray continuously and act upon God's prompting? It could mean the difference between a fulfilled life and just a regular, mundane existence. James 1:4-6 urges us to pray for wisdom if we lack it; and God, who is so merciful and generous, will reward us with wisdom. If you believe—and not doubt—God will provide the wisdom. Unfortunately, many people have not tapped into the power of prayer and have not recognized the need to ask for wisdom and discernment.

But most fulfilled, confident people live their lives following their instincts. It is intuitive to them. These individuals have answered the question, moved into the sweet spot, and been guided by God whose design is revealed in them. When we have the courage to leave the familiar and step into the destiny to which our instincts keep drawing us, we can live the same way.

I am not saying that tapping into your instincts will make you rich because I know that many rich people do not have keen instincts. I am not writing to say you will become famous by following your instincts. Too many famous people are miserable. I write to share with you the importance of being led into your fulfilled destiny by leaving the confines of your conventional cave and entering the open, sunny space where your heart longs to reside, where you will naturally hear your instincts and follow them.

It's a sad thing to live your life without this deep-rooted sense of connection to God's intention for your life. Like a light bulb without a lamp, this kind of disconnect fosters dark and foreboding feelings in the soul. Whether you are the manager or the employee, the homemaker or the home builder, what matters most is that you have been awakened to your godly design and enlightened to the inner fulfillment that it affords.

The place you will discover when instinct is your guide is far more fulfilling than any place you've been. Think of the fashion designers who do what they do beyond the training they received, with an inherent, instinctive flair for the latest trends. Interior decorators and graphic artists may wield this gift as well, but they are not the only ones. Athletes in the "zone," investors with a keen sense of timing, performers with the courage to audition for a role outside their fans' expectations all know what it means to function by their own unique internal compass.

Once you embrace the concept of following your inborn drive and begin to realize your potential, you better understand why you are so shaped and designed. You can now see why you were rejected in other places, why you grew bored in other roles, and why over and over you were haunted by the possibility that there's some place, some plan, some design to which you should be aligned.

Tap into your most powerful tool for recognizing instinct—prayer. And watch God lead you to a more fulfilling life.

✪ ✪ ✪ ✪

Prayer
Prayer answering God, I ask for your guidance and wisdom to help me live my life instinctively. Uncover my deepest passions and purpose so I might live a fulfilled and blessed life serving you and others.
In Jesus' name. Amen.

4

FLIP THE SCRIPT

*We humans keep brainstorming options and plans, but
GOD's purpose prevails.*
Proverbs 19:21, MSG

Do you ever wonder what most successful people
have in common? What fuels their engines and
makes them do what they do? Many successful
people are trailblazers—people who were not afraid to
take a detour from well-planned, scripted lives. They set
out and took risks that were not on their five-year plan.
They weren't afraid to leave the cages of comfort or the
scripted plans to head into the wilds of judicious risk and
discovery. The job they took wasn't on their list. The new
career wasn't a part of their plans. Going back to school,
starting an organization or business wasn't in their view;
but their instinct told them it was the right time and they
should follow a new path.

These trailblazers—many who set out on a different

path well after they were well on in years—followed a path that others would not. They took a detour in life and pursued something that wasn't completely laid out. All of these detours were either guided by instinctive decisions or somehow these trailblazers learned to incorporate an instinctive move that lifted them above their peers.

How is this done? In life, we all tend to make plans. The college student is often asked what they would like to be doing in five years or ten years. Newlyweds often have plans for their marriage, such as when they'd like to begin a family or purchase a home. Good business people make plans involving earnings and growth projections or vision statements that show how they'd like their product or services to develop and expand.

But what happens when a new opportunity becomes available? Can you forgo your preconceived plans and follow the new path? Or will you try to make what you have envisioned work? Could you try the different approach even though it wasn't in your plans?

It's not an easy answer, nor is it cut and dry. But this is where God-given instinct comes strongly into play. A trailblazer isn't afraid to pray about a move, a change in their plans.

Christian trailblazers realize and fully understand the Scripture that says we make plans, but God's purpose prevails. It is good to have plans. It is good to have an idea of where you want to be or what you want your business to do. It is foolish not to have a plan, an idea of where you want to go and what you want to do. If you don't, you're a drifter. But even with those well-laid plans, can you trust God when your instincts lead you in a new direction or to a new opportunity? Can you have faith to take a detour and follow the path that is unchartered, unprecedented, or not what you had figured out?

Trailblazers must have faith; they must move by instinct. They follow the inward urging even if it is not what they've written in their journals or business plans.

A person who is following their instinct will learn to discern opportunities and discern when God may be directing them to follow a different path. Truly, an instinct follower understands that God's purposes prevail, regardless of all of the brainstorming and plotting and planning. Instinct followers want to have their steps ordered by God so they will follow God's prompting—even if it's not in the plans, even if it's not written down, even if they can't download all of the points on the GPS. Trailblazers know when it's time to forgo their plans to follow God's purpose and plans. And they are ready!

Prayer
Gracious God, teach me to hold my plans lightly and to
offer them up to you. Give me wisdom to know when
to stop and when to go. I desire to follow you and your
plans more than anything.
Amen.

5

EVOLVE INTO SUCCESS

And we know that God causes everything to work together for the good of those who love God and are called according to his purpose for them.
Romans 8:28, NLT

Another common denominator of successful people is evolution. Most successful people did not grow up or develop in an environment of success. They evolved into their achievements. It's almost as if their obscure lives led them to be successful. Obscurity preceded their accomplishment much like a mother who pushes through and births a child.

It could come as a surprise to you, but giving a child everything he or she dreams of doesn't necessarily create skills and ambitions in a kid. Those whose parents lack resources—poorer or less-indulged kids—are forced to imagine, develop, and create in ways that a child with lots of resources is not.

Being poor—or lacking some things—can make you desire different and more. Having limited resources can lead you to observe and imagine. And if it is channeled well, need can be an impetus for success. Everyone has a different story. But often those of us who didn't grow up with silver spoons in our mouths develop an instinct for success. Our less than ideal circumstances ignite a special flame, produce a hunger for more, and serve as a catalyst to seek something different.

While instinct is instilled in us at birth, learning to listen to it evolves from our life's experiences—from lack or even from exposure to much.

So don't curse your humble beginnings, your less than stellar beginnings, or whatever your circumstances. And if you were born into comfort and given it all, don't despair that God has no special assignment for you. God is such an awesome designer and creator that he can help you use those experiences and observations to catapult you to success by following your inborn drive.

What have you been through? What makes you happy or unhappy? Often our passions come from the things that get us excited or upset; it's often the same side of the coin. When we use everything that has been deposited within us, whether intentionally or unintentionally, we have the inner workings that can drive us to achieve more and to obtain success. How we process our experiences influences our instincts. So instead of finding reasons why you can't be successful or rehashing the particulars of your past, see them as a catalyst for bringing you to this point. See each experience as God weaving together your life's journey and story to bring out your inner gifts, skills, and inclinations.

Romans 8:28 makes it clear that things can work together to bring about good. Not everything is good, but everything can work toward good. Instead of being upset about how things are or how things were, remember that God might be weaving together all of those experiences to produce something good inside of you that can come out and do good in the world. Pay attention to all of the paths you've been down and all of the paths you go down. Whether they seem good or bad, allow God to use them for good.

You'll eventually see how your instincts were uniquely formed and developed and how they led you on your distinct path.

✿ ✿ ✿ ✿

Prayer
My Heavenly Hope, thank you for each of my experiences—the good, bad, and ugly. Help me to see how they have worked together to make me who I am and to create instincts inside of me. Help me to use those instincts to unleash what is innately inside of me and who you've called me to be and what you've called me to do. Thank you for working things together for my good.
In Jesus' name. Amen.

6

GIFTS COME FROM GOD

*Every good and perfect gift is from above, coming down
from the Father of the heavenly lights, who does not change
like shifting shadows.*

James 1:17, NIV

Our instincts are here to do more than just make us successful. Our instincts don't exist merely to enhance our experience here on earth. Our gifts should serve as constant reminders that God has placed into us all that we need. Our gifts should point back to the giver, God.

Think of it this way: What God has given us is our gift. How we use that gift is what we give back to God. And this operates in areas far beyond ministry.

We see people offering their gifts back to God in various ways: a poet who can turn words into inspiration; a singer who can lift a person's spirit through song; or a teacher who can inspire a child. Think about the business leader who develops a big corporation that provides jobs for many and services for more. Think about the architect who builds a building designed to handle the specific purpose of the structure. All of their gifts are not being used just to glorify themselves. In fact, the individuals are sometimes secondary to their gifts. They use their God-given gifts to help others. It's a gift back to God.

We all have been instinctively prewired with a gift or several gifts from God. It's what makes you you and not your brother or sister. Scripture reminds us that our gifts are from God. Everything that is good and perfect comes from God and should be used to glorify God by helping others.

Have you tapped into your natural gift? Have you treated it like a gift from God? Have you cherished it, honed it, perfected it, and are you continuing to perfect it? Or do you treat it like a burden? Do you shy away from what you know you should be doing? Do you downplay your gift, considering it not worthy of glory?

Consider a hospital and all it takes to make it work. If it was filled with only doctors, who would check us in, who would get the charts ready, and who would smile and greet us with an assuring glance when we entered the building? Who would make sure the instruments were clean and sterile? Who would clean the restrooms so we'd have a comfortable place to refresh ourselves? Who would prepare the meals for patients, staff, and visitors?

See how everyone working together makes a vital place

like a hospital run? So you are to treat your gift—whether it is your JOB or not—with the ultimate respect. Work it and use it for God's glory and to help others.

❄ ❄ ❄ ❄

Prayer
Generous God, thank you for my gift. Thank you for
instilling it in me. Help me to respect it and develop it
and use it to glorify you.
Amen.

7

PASSIONS AND HATE

One day, after Moses had grown up, he went out to where
his own people were and watched them at their hard labor.
He saw an Egyptian beating a Hebrew, one of his own
people. Looking this way and that and seeing no one, he
killed the Egyptian and hid him in the sand. The next day he
went out and saw two Hebrews fighting. He asked the one in
the wrong, "Why are you hitting your fellow Hebrew?"
Exodus 2:11-13, NIV

The LORD said to him [Moses], "Who gave human beings
their mouths? Who makes them deaf or mute? Who gives
them sight or makes them blind? Is it not I, the LORD? Now
go; I will help you speak and will teach you what to say."
Exodus 4:11-12, NIV

Sometimes we have trouble identifying our highest
passion and gift. It's important to understand that oftentimes you can find your passions not just in what
you love, but also in what you passionately hate. Obvious-

ly, some people's passion is exemplified in what they love to do. Their personal preferences and professional proclivities make their positive passions easy to detect. But what you cannot stand is also a clue.

Think of Moses' example. He was born a Hebrew. He was Hebrew in every sense of the word; but he was raised, for all intents and purposes, an Egyptian. He lived in the king's palace. He grew up culturally as an Egyptian; but still, at his core, in his heart, he knew he was a Hebrew. And part of his passion surfaced in how he related to Hebrews—even though he could "pass" as an Egyptian. He had an intense passion for Hebrew people and a strong hatred for their mistreatment. See what he did when he saw an Egyptian beating a Hebrew? He passionately hated to see Hebrews being mistreated—by an Egyptian or by a fellow brother. He was so passionate about Hebrew mistreatment that it's noted in the Bible that he interfered at least twice (Exodus 2:11-13).

So it's no wonder God chose Moses to lead the Hebrews out of the oppressive Egypt. Even if Moses thought he was inadequate, God knew Moses' heart and special concern for the Hebrews. Moses was created to lead God's people out of bondage. What an honor! What an amazing task he was commissioned to do—because of his hatred for their mistreatment, because of his passion!

The same could be true for you; your passion could lie in what you love to hate. If you can't stand to see bad hairdos, maybe you should consider becoming a stylist. If you loathe seeing dilapidated houses and peeling paint, then maybe you should consider being a contractor or interior designer. Does the plight of the homeless make you shudder? Your passion might lead you to work with a nonprofit to eradicate this pervasive problem.

Your passion is your instinctive power. Knowing what you love, as well as what you love to hate, can fuel your instincts in ways that provide a super-octane boost to the engine of your success.

Prayer

Almighty God, thank you for my God-given passions. I will look for my passions throughout my days in the things I love and adore as well as in the things I passionately hate. I trust you to show me how to channel my energies to follow my passions and to do your will.

Amen.

8

MUCH IS REQUIRED

Every one to whom much is given, of him will much be required.

Luke 12:48b, RSV

At first read, the parable Jesus tells of the faithful and wise manager (Luke 12:35-48) can be startling. It seems rather harsh. A master leaves his estate to his servants to care for. If he returns and finds the servants doing what they are supposed to, he will be happy. He will even promote the servant to a higher position. But if the master returns and find servants being lax or throwing parties or just not taking care of the business at hand, surely those servants will receive severe punishments. And those who knew what to do but didn't do it will receive the harshest punishment.

But the crux of the parable gives us good news. It says: "From everyone who has been given much, much will be demanded." What this parable highlights is that God won't measure us by some unrealistic, man-made set of rules or compare us to someone else. God is not expecting us to operate under someone else's plans or weighing us on someone else's scale.

Each of us is called to do just what God has individually instructed us to do. If the Almighty has given us several gifts, we are expected to use several gifts. We are expected to take care of those gifts, develop them, nurture them, and use them for good. Likewise, if we are given even more gifts, we should be doing even more with our gifts. It's a call to faithfulness. It's a call to recognize that a gift is a gift and the proper response when you receive a gift is: "Thank you." To say: "Thank you, but so-and-so got more" or "Thank you, but I really wanted the gift you gave her" is wrong. We simply say: "Thank you" and use our gift well to show God our gratitude.

How are you saying thank you to God for whatever God has instilled in you? Are you truly developing your gift—however many you have? Or are you still wondering why your brother or sister got more or something different? It's not your business what anyone else has; you only are required to take care of what the Master has put under your charge. You are required to use what you have been given—nothing more, nothing less.

Your proper response is to thank God through cherishing and developing and using your gift—however large or small it may be. You've got to use your gift and reinforce your instincts with determination and perseverance. It is required.

So stop focusing on others and focus on what God has given you. Focus on what God has called you to do. We're not called to use others as a barometer. We're called to maximize the fullness of what God has uniquely entrusted to us.

❁ ❁ ❁ ❁

Prayer
Almighty God, I want to act according to what you have given me. Forgive me for comparing myself to others. I desire to use the gifts you have given me to say thank you.
In Jesus' name. Amen.

USE WHAT YOU GOT

*For to everyone who has, more will be given, and he will
have abundance; but from him who does not have, even
what he has will be taken away.*
Matthew 25:29, NKJV

Jesus' teachings are filled with treasures on how to live
instinctively. And in this parable, we find another
seemingly harsh illustration. (Matthew 25:14-29). The
parable shows how a man left his three servants with three
different amounts of money, which is described as talents—a unit of weight and money. We get the current use
of the word meaning gift or skill from this parable of *talents*. The man who had received the most talents (five) invested his master's money and gained five more for a total
of ten to return to his master. The second man, who had
received two, did the same thing. He doubled the master's
money by making two more for a total of four. But, the
servant who only received one did absolutely nothing to

add value to that one. Scripture says that servant dug a hole in the ground and hid that one talent.

When the master returns and inspects all that his servants have done, he is pleased with the first two servants. He tells each of them, "Well done, good and faithful servant! You have been faithful with a few things; I will put you in charge of many things. Come and share your master's happiness!" But the master is angry when he finds that third servant has done nothing with his talent, which again is a metaphor for gifts. The servant's explanation for his lackluster performance is: "I knew that you were a hard man, harvesting where you have not sown and gathering where you have not scattered seed. So I was afraid and went out and hid your talent in the ground." The master then takes that one talent, that one gift, from the third servant and gives it to the one who already had made ten talents.

Harsh consequences? Think again. This parable clearly shows what God expects from his children, all of whom he has given various gifts of varying amounts. We all have God-given gifts and talents. Some may have gifts that we can see easily and readily—like performers. Others have supportive gifts that are less visual—the organizer, administrator, production staff. But all of these are gifts. And all of these gifts should be used to help God's people, which in turn gives God glory.

If God has given you five gifts, take those talents and gifts and instinctively use them to make gifts to God. If

God has given you one gift, by no means should you hide it. Use your small, minor gift for all its worth! As Dr. Martin Luther King, Jr. said: "Be a bush if you can't be a tree."

Those who live by instinct know that they can't hide their talents or gifts. They know they've been called to use every bit they have. They know you have to seize the opportunities—whatever they may be—and have the courage to forge into the unknown. They maximize every gift they are given.

What are you doing with your gifts, talents, and resources? Are you using them and multiplying them? Or are you sitting and comparing them to the gifts that have been given to others, saying what you don't have or stuck on what you wish you had?

There's no time like now to use what you've got to do what needs to be done.

Prayer
God, the giver of every gift, thank you for each of my talents. Forgive me for trying to hide them. I vow from this day forth to use and invest them so that they will multiply and give you glory.
Amen.

10

FEAR OF FAILURE

*"Then the man who had received one bag of gold came.
'Master,' he said, 'I knew that you are a hard man, harvesting where you have not sown and gathering where you have
not scattered seed. So I was afraid and went out and hid
your gold in the ground. See, here is what belongs to you.'"*
Matthew 25:24-25, NIV

People who live fulfilling lives following their instincts
have learned to overcome their fear of failure. These
successful and happy people have learned to handle
their fears. In fact, they've learned to put them in check.

The powerful parable about the servants with the bags
of gold, or talents, illustrates how fear can hinder us. Consider the servant who hid his talent.

This man with one talent or bag of gold or gift told his
master that he was afraid to do anything with that one talent. Instead, he chose to hide it in the ground. He buried
it. He decided not to use it, not to multiply it, not to invest
it. He chose to hide it. This man said he was afraid of the

master; he knew he was a hard and tough man. So, instead of using the one gift he had, this man gave into fear and hid that one talent. He was afraid. And fear won.

The issue here is his fear of failure. His fear of disappointing the hard task master made him hide the gold. His fear of failure compelled him to hide what he'd been given rather than risk it for increase. He hid his talent and exposed his fear, instead of hiding his fear and exposing his talent. He allowed his fear to surface and take control of what he did.

Instinctively successful people have learned to live with fear. They step out regardless. They follow their instincts regardless of the fear.

When I gave my first sermon, I was shaking. I had to hide my hands to keep the audience from seeing them tremble. Had I given into my fear, I may not have ever preached that sermon or another one after that. But because I instinctively recognized that God had given me a gift—a gift I needed to use to help others—I pushed past my fear and preached again and again and again. I hid my fear and God exposed my talents.

Name whatever you are afraid of. Identify what is holding you back from following your instincts and developing your gifts to bless others. Tap into your faith by reading God's Word, the Bible. Seek God's help to conquer fear via prayer. We have an unspoken responsibility that comes with the gifts that we each have been given. Even if you are afraid, stand up any way. Even if you are shaking, do it any way. Follow your instinct and step out on faith.

Allow God to empower you to do what you've been called to do—whatever that may be. People are waiting; it is your responsibility. Don't let fear make you hide your talent.

Prayer
Most merciful God, please forgive me for allowing fear
to make me hide the gifts you have given me. Help me to
trust you and step out on faith. Help me to use my gifts
responsibly and without fear.
Amen.

11

GOD'S STANDARD

*Again, it will be like a man going on a journey, who called
his servants and entrusted his wealth to them. To one he
gave five bags of gold, to another two bags, and to another
one bag, each according to his ability.*
Matthew 25:14-15a, NIV

Another critical point in the parable of the talents
is that God has given us instincts so we don't have
to copy another person's talents and gifts. God
holds each of us to a unique standard, and we must accept
responsibility for its fulfillment. We don't have to imitate
anyone else's success, but we do have to invest our talents
in the dreams we've been given. If you read the entire parable, you will see that the master didn't give any instructions when he left his servants with talents. I imagine
again they had to use instinct to determine the best way
to invest them.

Unfortunately, there's no instruction manual in the box

when you uncrate the gift inside of you. I can't tell you how many times I wished there were some type of specific directions given to explain exactly how we should use our tangible and intangible gifts. The singer has the gift of song but no sheet music revealing whether to teach, perform, or record. The artist has the gift of drawing, but there is no clear blueprint as to whether he should pursue graphic design or fine art landscapes.

If instructions were included with our gifts, then our instincts would not have to be activated. God doesn't give details when he gives gifts. He just gives us the instinct and the opportunity. He allows us to meet the right people at the right time who challenge us with how they perceive our capacity to perform. When life gives us an opportunity to use our gifts, this is our permission to advance.

Don't wait on someone else to tell you how, when, and where to do what only you can know inside you. No one will tell you: this is the moment. No announcer will declare: this is the opportunity you've been waiting for. No parent, spouse, business partner, mentor, lover, coach, teacher, or pastor can tell you the time of your appointment with destiny.

Instead there is only an instinct of urgency. There is an instinct of necessity. There is a still small voice that says, "This is the moment right now!"

I've often had people write me on Facebook or Twitter and ask, "How do I know what I'm created to do?" I have a habit of looking at the profile of people who pose this question. More times than not, I am expecting a college student or a high school sophomore to be the one asking such questions. But that's not usually the case. Many times people in their forties and fifties are still standing over the box of life trying to find the directions as to how they should put together the gifts they have been given.

Many spend their entire lives at the crossroads of greatness trying to decipher which way they should go. They do not know that the longer they deliberate the more they lose. The singer loses his voice with age. The runner's legs get stiff as time passes. The business environment changes with the ebb and flow of the economy. Lost time means irretrievably lost opportunities.

Don't get caught like the man with one talent. He didn't receive instructions for using his talent and didn't use his instinct to figure it out.

Imagine what could have happened if he stepped out on faith, trusting his instincts.

✪ ✪ ✪ ✪

Prayer
Loving God, thank you for my gifts—each of them and all of them. I commit myself to have faith enough to hear your unique call on my life to activate each of the gifts you've placed inside of me. I want to make good return on your gift.
In Jesus' name. Amen.

12

THE REWARD

*"His master replied, 'Well done, good and faithful servant!
You have been faithful with a few things; I will put you in
charge of many things. Come and share your master's happiness!'"*

Matthew 25:23, NIV

Doesn't it blow your mind how much you can
glean from one passage of Scripture? Let's take
one more look at the parable of the talents (also
known as bags of gold). Jesus had much to teach through
his parables and the lessons are still multiplying.

As we look at what the master said to each of the servants who multiplied their gifts, we notice he extends a
special invitation: "Come and share your master's happiness!" The servants had shattered the glass ceiling! They
had a chance, in spite of the normative constraints of the
time, to advance to the next dimension of living. This was
their crossover moment to go way beyond all previous pa-

rameters. They could now enjoy a change in status, experience the freedom that comes with a change in responsibility, rebrand who they were and how they lived.

This is how people excel. Not one of the servants took this as an opportunity to brag about what he could do. Each simply did what was in him to do. One returned with ten and the other with four. But each performed 100 percent at his level. Each under-promised and over-delivered. This is so vitally important that I'll say it again: you aren't in a race with a level of gifting that is beyond what you were given. Excellence is individual. The reward is based on what you do with what you have! The result of your authentic stewardship is always promotion.

The knock of opportunity, if answered with the right instinctive action, will inevitably result with promotion into the next dimension. Can you imagine when these stewards went back to their servant quarters and started shoving their meager personal effects into a bag thinking, "We're moving into the master's quarters—not as servants but as masters!" Such a moment would be too surreal to describe, too magical to articulate.

The intoxicating feeling of promotion is the entrance to the new opportunities of the next dimension. You, yourself are on the cusp of such a transition. Think back to a time when you have experienced this kind of growth. It's the kind of promotion that makes you drive home from work giggling to yourself in the car! It's the kind of advancement that brings joyful exuberance and confidence,

because you know you've done what only you can do—
you've given it your all and been recognized for it! This
kind of exhilaration causes the soul to soar. These moments may include financial advancement, but tangible
assets are not the greatest reward.

The greatest reward is the confirmation of what you
already knew instinctively. You've received an answer to
the haunting question forever dancing around the edges
of your mind. "Yes—I was made for more!" your reward
proclaims. It is the answer to the question that most of us
have within regarding our greater call, our greater destiny,
and some greater expectation beyond our circumstance.

The voice inside was right! The inclinations were authentic. My instinct was accurate. What started out as a
suspicion, a hypothesis, an intuition has now been con-
firmed. It changes our deepest perception of ourselves. It
transforms how others perceive us as well.

My hope is that these truths may be the tutoring you
need to prepare you for activating your instinct to increase. It's time for you to respond to the rapping fist of
opportunity's fierce knock on the door of your life right
now. If you will answer the knock and honor the chance
with discipline, creativity, and urgency, you may find
yourself—your true self—living a life that exceeds your
wildest dreams!

✪ ✪ ✪ ✪

Prayer

Masterful God, I welcome the opportunity to use each of my gifts to multiply. Help me follow my instincts as I place my faith in your unchanging hands. I look forward to hearing you say, "Well done, my good and faithful servant."

Amen.

13

TURN FAILURES INTO VICTORIES

Count it all joy, my brothers, when you meet trials of various kinds, for you know that the testing of your faith produces steadfastness. And let steadfastness have its full effect, that you may be perfect and complete, lacking in nothing.
James 1:2-4, ESV

How you handle failure is critical in living successfully. People who follow instincts are not immune to failure. Successful people have many failures, but they often view them differently than other people. Instinct followers know how to take those failures and make them lessons. They follow their instincts beyond the skinned knees, beyond the emotions of their failures.

Scripture tells us how to handle failure or trouble. We should be happy—glad—about them. James says that we should consider trials (failures) with pure joy. We don't jump for joy because we have failed, but there *is* special learning to be gained from failures. Trials and failures and hard times can test our faith. And when our faith is tested, we learn.

The same is true for those who follow their instincts, those who leave cages of comfort. If something doesn't work, we can learn from it. If we try something and we fail at it, we now have more information about the process. We can use that information the next time and the next time and the next time. Our failures become classrooms. Our failures give us the answer for next week's test.

It's not how many times you have failed; it's what you've learned each time you got back up on your feet. Toddlers don't start walking the first time they try. They stumble, bumble, trip, and sometimes hurt themselves when they try to walk. But they keep on trying. They keep getting back on their feet and tottering forward until they have mastered the skill.

How have you learned from your failures? Did losing that job a few years ago help you discover the kind of work environment where you can thrive? Did declaring bankruptcy for your home business enable you to manage your finances better for your new company? Each failure can point to future success. It really is all in how you handle it—how you decide to learn from the failure, not bury it or pretend it didn't happen or decide to give up.

In my book *Instinct: The Power to Unleash Your Inborn Drive*, I remind readers of what happened to me when I first started the play *Woman, Thou Art Loosed!* At first, it was a comedy of errors. Everything that could go wrong did go wrong. Ticket sales were so poor that we ended up giving away a large number of tickets just to fill the auditoriums we had booked. But I didn't give up. I used the failures as lessons. I learned that you open in small markets to work out the kinks of the show before you take the show to large cities. I learned which venues were better than others and which ones to avoid all together. I learned how to hire people who knew about these things. I even reached out to a young playwright and actor named Tyler Perry and asked him to help me with the script for my play. I didn't let how this venture started out stop me from trying and learning and trying again.

Consider your failures as great lessons. Rejoice in them, knowing that they can produce some valuable lessons. Don't let them keep you down, but instead put those lessons into action for the future. Your instincts will lead you and show you the way to go.

Prayer

Creator of the universe, thank you for the lessons along the way. Forgive me for cursing my trials and failures. Help me to see those times as golden opportunities to learn more about you and follow my instincts. Help me to put those lessons into action. I thank you for always picking me up when I fall down.

In Jesus' name. Amen.

14

ADVISORS

Plans fail for lack of counsel, but with many advisers they succeed.

Proverbs 15:22, NIV

While following our inborn drive, we may sometimes begin to think that it is all in the gut; it's all about what we feel. But true instinct followers know the importance of advisors. Successful people consider information from many sources and from a variety of sources. Your instincts and intelligence—the data and information we can get from advisors and other sources—need to work together. Instincts and intelligence work best when they have a collaborative exchange. Instincts can initiate the process that information validates. And Scripture reminds us of the importance of a variety of counsel, those who may have insight and experience we do not have.

While you may not implement all of the advice from everyone—and you shouldn't—you can benefit from having a variety of thoughts on the subject matter. For example, I have learned that I am instinctively a consultative leader. A person who uses this leadership style instinctively listens to feedback from the team and will ultimately make a decision, but not without consulting all available influences to ascertain a course of action that is collaborative.

We gain intelligence from multiple perspectives. We often miss important information when we surround ourselves with one type of person or with people who look and think and act just like we do. Reread the story I retell in *Instinct* of the elephant and the four blind men (p. 197).

Each of the blind men touched a different part of the large animal. One of them touched his massive ears and said, "This beast is flat and flexible—like a palm leaf." Then the second man touched the elephant's huge legs and said, "No, he is sturdy and round like a tree trunk." Still, the third man touched the elephant's tail and said, "You both are wrong. This creature is thin and wiry like a snake." And the fourth man leaned in and touched the side of the elephant. He said, "You all are wrong. This animal is strong and sturdy, like a stone wall."

Advisors can help us gain multiple perspectives. And relying only on one person or one source of information can keep us trapped and make us miss the real picture. If we would accept only one of the blind men's perspectives, we wouldn't have a true picture of what an elephant is like. But if we combine all four of the men's perspectives—even with their blind spots—we have a broader, more global, and much more comprehensive view of our mammoth friends.

Who is on your personal and professional advisory boards? You may not have a formal board that meets every quarter, but you should know who you can go to for advice and information. Is that board comprised of members who look just like you, act like you, have the same background as you? If your board is not coming from multiple perspectives, you may be missing out on some important sides of your elephant. You need multiple points of view in order to see the big picture.

Allow your multitude of advisors to help you move forward on what your instincts have prompted. They can be your litmus test to evaluate your instincts, which can help your plans succeed.

✪ ✪ ✪ ✪

Prayer
Wonderful Counselor, thank you for creating so many different people with so many unique gifts and perspectives. You are amazing. Lead me to tap into the multitude of ideas and resources you have given me. I commit to seeking a variety of advisors to share my thoughts and plans so that I may wisely follow my inborn instincts.
Amen.

15

USE YOUR OWN TOOLS

Then Saul dressed David in his own tunic. He put a coat of armor on him and a bronze helmet on his head. David fastened on his sword over the tunic and tried walking around, because he was not used to them. "I cannot go in these," he said to Saul, "because I am not used to them." So he took them off. Then he took his staff in his hand, chose five smooth stones from the stream, put them in the pouch of his shepherd's bag and, with his sling in his hand, approached the Philistine.

1 Samuel 17:38-40, NIV

Many people trip and fall when trying to follow their gifts because they are trying to copy the way someone else is doing it or has done it. These people believe that in order to be successful, they need to follow a set formula and do things just the way someone else did them. This is not instinctive. This is copying.

What these people fail to understand is that we are all

created uniquely and instinct is distinctly woven into the very fiber of our DNA, our special code. You can't do your thing the exact same way as someone else does it. And when we don't do our thing, we're depriving the world of our uniqueness, of experiencing what God has put into us in a unique way.

God does not ask you to compare yourself to someone else or do exactly what someone else does, exactly how that person does it.

Consider David when he stood up to the challenge of knocking down the Israelites' taunter, the giant Goliath. David had already been nurturing his God-given gift of protecting sheep. He had honed his gift and skills by warding off bears and lions. He probably had never put on armor before. So when Saul gave David this heavy coat of armor and this big bronze helmet to protect his head, David couldn't walk. Saul's tools paralyzed David. He couldn't function like he instinctively knew he could if he didn't have this heavy suit on.

David was in tune with his own ability. He knew how God helped him slay large animals before—without any armor. So David didn't try to use the same tools that Saul or any of the warriors would have used. David used his own tools—a simple sling and five smooth stones. He had success because he was bold enough to know that he couldn't fight the way the rest of the men were fighting. Their armor couldn't be his armor. He had a different gift, and he was bold enough to use it.

Instinct followers know that they have special gifts and skills. They know what uniqueness they bring to a project or a business. They do not spend countless hours trying to emulate someone else for the sake of emulating. They know that won't work. Instead, they tap into their gifts and use them to succeed—even if their neighbor is using something else. Instinct followers understand that we are not called to use others as a barometer of our breakouts or even as a barometer of how something should be done. We're called to maximize the fullness of what God has uniquely entrusted to us!

We use our exposure to others as fuel, but not as the engine itself. Others empower our self-discovery and energize our instincts, but we don't borrow their ways. Remember, our DNA is different for a reason. You were created as you with your gift and skills. I was created as me with my gifts and skills. If we all get in tune with our instinctive gifts, together we will make a difference.

Prayer
Awesome Creator, you created me as you saw fit, and I commit myself to use my inborn gifts to glorify you. I will resist the temptation to use someone else's tools and will cultivate what you have already given me.
In Jesus' name. Amen.

16

DISCERNMENT

The discerning heart seeks knowledge.
Proverbs 15:14a, NIV

And this I pray, that your love may abound still more and more in knowledge and all discernment, that you may approve the things that are excellent, that you may be sincere and without offense till the day of Christ,
Philippians 1:9-10, NKJV

Discernment is another way to think of instinct. This quiet—and intangible—skill is power-packed and able to guide you in ways that intellect alone just can't.

Discernment is the something inside of you that tells you to go right. It's the thing inside of you that tells you it is the right time to make your move. It's the thing inside of you that tells you to give someone a chance who might not ordinarily seem like the best one for the gig. Now discernment doesn't throw away intelligence; discernment doesn't operate without intelligence and facts. Discernment seeks the proper balance between knowledge and instinct. Discerning hearts seek to balance wisdom and intellect, the internal sense with knowledge, while a rash person disregards one for the other.

Another way to look at discernment is as deeper understanding. It's not surface stuff. It goes beyond what can meet the eye and can just about go straight to the heart of the matter. Discernment has a way of peeling back the outward layers and seeing the core—the real deal of the matter, person, or situation.

The wise person seeks to discern the right time and the right opportunities. They know that intellect alone isn't enough. They pray for wisdom and for God to incline their hearts to know when and how to execute. Instinct helps wise people know the more excellent way. It's not just about knowing the facts; it's about understanding. Wise people know how to tap into their inner sense that guides them and gives them information that intellect alone just can't provide.

Meditate on the decisions you've made recently. Did you use intelligence and facts alone to make the decision, or were you able to tap inside and draw upon understanding to better comprehend the situation? Decide today to seek more understanding when making decisions. Follow your instinct to go directly to the core of the matter. Your heart will lead the way.

✿ ✿ ✿ ✿

Prayer
Great discerner of spirits, thank you for intellect and
thank you for instincts. Thank you for discernment.
Continue to guide me to find the more excellent way so
that I may execute the plans you have designed for my
life. I am eternally grateful.
Amen.

17

BALANCE INSTINCTS AND INTELLECT

We humans make plans, but the LORD has the final word. We may think we know what is right, but the LORD is the judge of our motives. Share your plans with the LORD, and you will succeed.

Proverbs 16:1-3, CEV

The powerful story of the zoologist and Zulu on my South African safari changed my perspective. This real-life metaphor gave me amazing new insight into what makes some people stand out and live successfully while others don't. It's not purely intelligence or even hard work. We all know some very smart people who do not experience the joy-filled satisfaction others do. Why? Perhaps the smart people allowed themselves to take risks only when the information lined up. Perhaps they have so much data, so much information, or so much intelligence that they are not in tune with their instinct. They don't know when to jump based on an inner sense. Instead they are still waiting on the data to say that jumping makes sense.

I like to think of this as planning to a fault. Plans are great. Plans are needed. We need proper information to inform our decisions. But an instinct follower recognizes that information isn't all you need. Even the zoologist recognized picking up the Zulu on the safari would help us to find the elephants. While the zoologist knew about the elephants; the Zulu knew about instincts. And smart people can know a whole lot; smart people can plan a whole lot. But those looking for godly success know that God put something unique inside all of us that will make us know when something is right or wrong.

This thing called instinct is one thing that college degrees and on-the-job experience cannot instill in you. Your professors and bosses can invest countless hours exposing you to critical information and inspiring you with historical empirical data that will be invaluable as you trek through life. But the gift they cannot give you is the instinct to know when to do what only you can do and where to do it!

In order to harness your intentions with your actions, you must rely on instincts. Every visionary learns that they must be well-informed and well-equipped to accomplish their targeted achievements. But they must also be in touch with their instincts in order to use their experience, education, and equipment to fulfill their expectations. Instincts can help connect the dots between where you're trying to go and how you will get there.

Intellect can make a salesman knowledgeable about his product, but it cannot tell him how to read his client. The police academy can teach an officer about crime scenes, but it cannot teach him how to search his gut and go with his instincts. The dating service can bring the right age, IQ, and physical attributes of a possible spouse before you from its extensive database, but it can't accurately measure the actual chemistry that will exist between you and your prospective mate when you finally meet.

Instincts can tell you when you are on to something or when you are just going for a ride. Instincts can help you when hiring a new employee or closing a business deal. When you learn to follow your instincts, you can advance from being someone who knows to someone who knows how to execute.

Rather than rely solely on your intellect, learn to listen to your inner voice and wisdom.

✪ ✪ ✪ ✪

Prayer
Loving God, thank you for instincts. Thank you for the inner drive that provides special information that intellect alone can't give me. I will rely on you to show me when to follow my instincts. I am grateful.
Amen.

18

HEAD, HEART, AND INSTINCT

The wisdom of the wise keeps life on track.
Proverbs 14:8a, MSG

A commonsense person lives good sense.
Proverbs 13:16a, MSG

In order to travel at our maximum velocity, we must balance the power of our intellect with the truth of our instincts, our information, and our wisdom. Each of these parts must perform well to help you advance and perform at your optimal potential. Many people live lives that are in poor rotation—like unbalanced tires on a car—which consequently impedes their mobility because they don't balance what they know with what they sense.

Information—or intelligence—in its purest form is irreplaceable in leadership as well as in life. Intelligence isn't merely one's IQ; it is also having the necessary access to relevant data and pertinent information, and the understanding to interpret it correctly. As essential as instincts are to exploring the design of your destiny, you must not ignore the facts for the feelings! Intelligence has its place and is vital even to your instincts.

However, instinct and discernment have their proper place too. Balancing what you know in your mind with what you know in your heart takes practice and intentionality. This kind of instinctive intelligence requires walking a tightrope between what is verifiable and what is intangible. Successful people use instinct with intellect to make each decision more useful. Without access to intelligence, one cannot develop successful strategies or create sensible solutions. And yet nothing you've read should replace your reliance upon instinct to inform the decisions you make. The two must work in sync—like the wheels on the car.

If your gut feeling contradicts the facts, then ask people you trust to weigh in before you ignore the objective information at hand. Use what you know and what you sense to arrive at a more synthesized decision, one that integrates both objective and subjective realities. It means using your head and your heart to follow your instinct, using information and discernment to get to the heart of the matter.

The two—intellect and discernment—can operate in isolation. While instincts may be the compass that gives direction, intelligence guides the process through which that transition can be realized. The proverbs say intelligent people (those who are wise or use commonsense) make good sense, or good decisions. They know to use intellect and discernment! No one can make great decisions if they have poor information. The greater your efforts to understand data, the more likely you are to liberate your instincts. On the other hand, always relying on the probability of progress by what appears on paper will not ensure success. Our instinct is informed by the data we feed it.

Not only does a wise person balance instincts with intellect, she must also make sure that the intelligence she's using comes from reliable sources with balanced perspectives. As you make decisions, consider what you are relying upon. Keep a healthy balance between the facts, information, or intelligence and the inner wisdom known as instinct. Observing and studying both instinct followers and intellectuals can provide information and help you discern.

Always considering yourself a student will help you balance the scales between intellect and instinct. A wise one always knows the need to keep the two in balance in order to stay on track in life.

✪ ✪ ✪ ✪

Prayer
All-knowing God, thank you for the reminder to balance intellect and instinct. I will always be a student, studying your Word, learning your will for my life. I will also use discipline to study and discern information around me.
In Jesus' name. Amen.

19

EAT FROM THE TOP

*They gave Moses this account: "We went into the land to
which you sent us, and it does flow with milk and honey!
Here is its fruit. But the people who live there are powerful, and the cities are fortified and very large. We even saw
descendants of Anak there. The Amalekites live in the Negev;
the Hittites, Jebusites and Amorites live in the hill country;
and the Canaanites live near the sea and along the Jordan."
Then Caleb silenced the people before Moses and said, "We
should go up and take possession of the land, for we can
certainly do it."*

Numbers 13:27-31, NIV

Some of the most valuable lessons I've learned at this
stage of my life were revealed or made clearer while
observing God's natural zoo in beautiful South Af-
rica.

While watching those long-necked, elegant giraffes
prance across God's artistic canvas, I noticed that giraffes
only eat the leaves at the top of the trees. The giraffes walk

the same plains as the other awesome animals we saw on safari and have access to the grass on the ground as well as the leaves on the short bushes, but these graceful long-legged creatures don't bother with the low-level foliage. They could bend their neck to reach anywhere they'd like. But they just stick to the treetops. They get their nutrients from the tip top of the trees.

That's what you have to do if you want to be successful. I'm not saying keep your nose in the air and think you're better than others. But you have to learn to eat—or find nourishment—from the places where you want to be. Many times we listen to people in lower places. People who don't live by instincts shouldn't have that much say in your life. Listen to those who are at different heights. You need affirmation and nourishment from those at your level or those who are at a higher level. They understand where you are trying to go and can help you.

Imagine if Moses had listened to the report of the majority in today's Scripture passage. What would have happened if Joshua and Caleb hadn't had faith to believe that God wanted the Hebrews to live in the Promised Land and said so? These faithful men surely wouldn't have been able to see the treetops if they had kept listening to the bottom feeders—those who couldn't see the opportunity because of the challenges.

In *Instinct*, I describe a time I gave up a big opportunity because I didn't learn from the giraffes early enough. I was asked to write a guest blog post on a new forum, a new arena—a place I could reach more people. I wrote the post, and I even let people that I admire read it before I submitted it. They agreed it was worthy of the brand of the notable forum. But when it was posted, the online comments poured in immediately. Most of the comments were rants and insults. Some attacked me as an individual (even though they don't know me or what I'm about). Others attached the topic of my post. Still others just wanted to vent—their comments didn't relate to what I had to say. I was distraught.

I decided to slowly back down from this new forum and stop contributing blog posts. But when I ran into the editor, she asked why I hadn't submitted more. I told her about the comments. She was shocked and told me my writings had been some of the highest-rated ones.

When I processed this conversation in light of the lessons that I learned from my tall giraffe friends, I realized that I had focused on the noise of the people who were not even the main audience. They were people who just wanted to vent or send attacks. The editor had told me that the forum's main audience was intellectuals who read the content but seldom left comments. She said she seldom read the comments after the article because those people often: "Just want to make noise; they have nothing of substance to say!"

Wow, I had let the noise makers keep me from pursuing a great opportunity. Never again. My giraffes have taught me where to get my affirmation and nourishment—from the top of the trees not from the bottom feeders.

Follow the giraffes and feed from the top. Get nourishment and affirmation from treetop dwellers, not bottom feeders.

✪ ✪ ✪ ✪

Prayer
Most Holy and Wonderful God, teach me to listen to constructive feedback and to ignore those who do not mean well. I desire to know the difference and to keep my focus on what you would have me to do.
In faith. Amen.

FEED YOUR HEART

For where your treasure is, there your heart will be also.
Matthew 6:21, NIV

Souls who follow their hearts thrive.
Proverbs 13:19a, MSG

L iving instinctively means feeding our core, our internal system that generates our passion. Our core
needs nourishment to thrive and grow and to survive. Whatever stimulates you and helps you be your best
self must be fed often for you to produce good and healthy
fruit.

The heart of a car is the engine. It doesn't matter if the
tires are glistening or how shiny the coat of paint is; if
there is no engine, the car is useless. Or if the engine is not
functioning properly, there will be problems. For it to run
properly and do what it is made to do, the heart of the car

has to be taken care of—even more than the coat of paint.

Consider where you put your most and best energy and whether it fuels your goals. Reflect on what is truly nourishing what is important to you. You may need to realign your priorities so your main goals are getting the nourishment they need. It may take some time to readjust; habits are not formed overnight. But pay attention to where your time and energy are going—and work to make sure the most important things are getting nourished, fed by you. When you have a healthy diet of nourishing your soul, you have more energy. When you have a healthy diet of nourishing your soul, you are happier and more fulfilled. In essence, when your soul is healthy, you are healthy.

In Matthew 6, Jesus reminds us about priorities. He says whatever we focus on will be our main thing. If your focus is just to get money, just to get rich, then that's what your main thing will be. That's where your heart will be. But if your focus is to use your gifts in a way that honors God, to use your passion to fuel your work, to follow your instincts so you can have fulfillment; then you will invest the time, money, and whatever is necessary to take care of your main thing, your focus. Your heart will be right where your true focus is when you live by instincts. And you will value heart-centered living.

So don't take your core and passion areas for granted. Don't take your marriage for granted. Don't take business colleagues for granted. Don't take the unique gift God has given you for granted. Feed your relationships. Nourish your gifts so what is really important to you can continue to pump blood to your heart. Invest in what's important to you.

Prayer
God in heaven, keep my focus on what you have called me to do. Show me how to nourish the gifts, the business, and the relationships you have given me. I know I need to nourish my core so that I can be my best.
Amen.

RAISE YOUR VISION

The glory of young men is their strength, gray hair the splendor of the old.

Proverbs 20:29, NIV

It is so fitting that giraffes eat from the tops of the trees, since that's what they see. Their turtle friends may be herbivores as well, but their sight lines are too low for a meaningful dialog with those twenty feet above them. And likewise, whenever you collide with people whose sight lines are limited by the view they have of the world, it's a futile exercise to expect them to see what you see.

Many people think like giraffes but eat like turtles. As a young twenty-something preacher, I encountered an older man from my church who asked what I thought he should do about his painful marriage. Truth be told, the complications of his relationship with his wife were far beyond my experience at the time. So after listening to him describe their issues with communication, trust, and jealousy, I hastily replied, "Divorce her."

Now before you judge me for my mistake, please realize that my young mind wasn't experienced with the hardships inherent in keeping a family afloat. My children were small, my wife was young, and my pastoral counseling experience limited. Needless to say, the man who sought my advice found it terribly adolescent. He was polite, but I could see the disappointment in his eyes.

We were living in two different worlds, we were planets in different orbits, and my counsel was limited by the space between us. He turned to me for wisdom, but I could not reach the point from which he was asking. As you can see, in this case, I was the turtle and he was the giraffe. My limited perspectives informed my worldview. I hadn't lived long enough to give a balanced view of what he should do.

Most of our opinions are based upon perspective. While you must respect everyone's right to offer an opinion, you cannot walk in the wisdom of someone who has never lived on your level. In short, a turtle and a giraffe can occupy the same habitat but they will never have the same sights! You can't wreck your neck to graze the grass, and he can't touch the treetops. Stay clear of his complaints and counsel. He is only reacting to his perspective.

Anyone who has lived very long shudders today at the ideas he had twenty years ago. Perspectives mature and ideas change as time and experiences allow you to find that what you thought in the grass seems ridiculous in the trees. Old age should bring wisdom, and the Bible does say gray hair brings splendor. So we should not discount the value of experience. Take a look at your counsel of advisors. It would be wise to have people who are older than you in age and in experience. While there is no doubt much to be learned from the younger, technologically savvy generation, don't forget about those who've already been down this path. Their perspectives can be enlightening.

One last note about the giraffe: It's remarkable that they aren't born with long necks. If they were, then birth would be unimaginable! God, in infinite wisdom, develops the giraffe's neck once it's outside the womb. Similarly, our necks grow with time and extend our views with experiences and opportunities that forever alter our perspectives.

✪ ✪ ✪ ✪

Prayer
Lord, I appreciate the perspective of those who gaze at the top level—whether from age or experience. I want to use wisdom and discernment when seeking counsel and advice. Guide me in the way you would have me to go.
Amen.

22

DAILY BREAD

Give us this day our daily bread.
Matthew 6:11, KJV

Now he who supplies seed to the sower and bread for food will also supply and increase your store of seed and will enlarge the harvest of your righteousness. You will be enriched in every way so that you can be generous on every occasion, and through us your generosity will result in thanksgiving to God.
2 Corinthians 9:10-11, NIV

Once you decide to tap into your instincts or commit to continuing to follow your instincts—the inclinations of the heart—you will realize that what you need most is inside you. Often the answers we seek from those around us are buried within us; we just have to pull them out. It's comforting to know that we have what we need. We have exactly what we need for this day, our daily bread. We have what we'll need to sustain us as we step out on faith and follow our inclinations.

When I reflect on the concept of resources rising to meet our need, I'm reminded of the blessing Moses gave to the tribe of Asher in Deuteronomy 33:25. The King James Version says: "...as thy days, so shall thy strength be." This literally means that in proportion to the demand, the resources will be there. So the greater your demand, the greater your resources will be. The more you need strength, the more strength will be available. The more prepared and ready you are for opportunities, the more opportunities will arise.

These needs may not always come when you want them—when you've planned for them to come. But just as the old folks said about God: "He may not come when you want him, but he's always on time." Exactly what you need will come exactly when you need it.

So my beloved, don't let fear of lack stop you from following your heart's inclinations. Pursue your God-given passions, develop your gifts; and what you need, what you think you lack will arise when it is needed. Test God and see. He is the supplier of the seed and the harvest! He gives the idea, and he can cause it to grow and multiply.

With the full armor of all that has been given to you, it's time to change the dynamics of the game. By living each day anticipating that God will provide your daily bread and your daily strength, you are in essence living as Jesus commanded. You are awaiting God to provide all you need, even the right time and right set of circumstances to make your inner resource arise for the challenge at hand. Don't be tempted to think too far ahead and fret over the mountain. By taking one day at a time, one step at a time, you are entrusting your journey to God's faithful and capable hands!

Your strength will be enough for this day!

Prayer
Jehovah Jireh, I believe your promise for strength for each day. I trust that all the resources I need are awaiting me, even inside of me. I will do everything in my power to follow my heart. I praise you forever.
Amen.

23

GET READY FOR CHANGE

To every thing there is a season, and a time to every purpose under the heaven: A time to be born, and a time to die; a time to plant, and a time to pluck up that which is planted; A time to kill, and a time to heal; a time to break down, and a time to build up.

Ecclesiastes 3:1-3, KJV

One of the most often heard phrases of a dying business, church, dream, or relationship is: "We've never done it that way." Even successful people who follow their God-given instincts can fall into detrimental patterns and resist the ever-present need to adapt and change. The failure to change and adapt to the times can cause all of your success and hard work to wither, dry up, or become totally irrelevant.

It is a challenge to stay vigilant to changes around you and adjust or even discard old ideas and concepts that have outlived their usefulness. It took me almost two years to realize that sending paper letters was not as effective as emails. I assumed our partners needed to receive their traditional, hard copy, paper letters until I noticed that we were mailing letters, but people were emailing us back.

A person who is truly in touch with their instincts eventually knows when change is necessary.

Sometimes change requires that we reach out to new people with different resources. Getting in touch with our instincts lets us know what we do well and what we can't do well. A wise person partners with people whose skills are different from theirs—skills that compliment theirs.

A friend of mine couldn't adapt to the change needed in her business. She started baking cookies in her home kitchen. When the business grew, she moved to an industrial kitchen she rented. Her cookies then received attention and were sold on a TV network. This new exposure led to so many orders that she couldn't fill them all. She needed to expand and get manufacturing and distribution help, but she was afraid of this big change. She needed investors, but this intimidated her. Instead of adapting to the changing needs of her business, she decided to walk away from a big opportunity. Change scared her.

Wise people know that everything has a season. There's a time to expand and a time to hold back. Don't hold on to the old just because it is familiar. Consistently evaluate those people and things around you to see if you still need them in the same capacity you once did. If you do, great. If you don't, consider a shift—a change. There could be something else or something different for them to do, or a new program or new place for you to work and grow.

Change doesn't always mean letting things go, but it does mean facing reality and making adjustments where needed. Look for your seasons of change and ask, as Scripture reminds us: Is it time to give birth? Is it time to let some things die? Perhaps it is time to plant? Maybe it is time to harvest. Still other times it is time to end a chapter or mend a relationship. It could be time to break things down or invest in building them up.

Whatever season you find yourself in, embrace it, assess what needs to be done, and follow the inclinations in your heart. Your instincts can lead you to the right place and help you prepare for a new season.

Get ready!

Prayer
Gracious God, you reign in every season of life, whether it is a time to start or a time to finish. I want to be in tune with you in the seasons in my life, and through Christ who gives me strength I will have the courage to make adjustments.
In Jesus' name. Amen.

24

PEOPLE CHANGE TOO

When I was a child, I talked like a child, I thought like a child, I reasoned like a child. When I became a man, I put the ways of childhood behind me. For now we see only a reflection as in a mirror; then we shall see face to face. Now I know in part; then I shall know fully, even as I am fully known.

1 Corinthians 13:11-13, NIV

Change can be a touchy concept, and it needs to be handled with much care—as delicately as balancing intellect and instinct. Your core values seldom need adjustment. These are the ethical ideologies that define who you are. But if you do not make adjustments, if you do everything the way you did when you started out, you're not growing. The meaning doesn't change, but the method must always evolve; and sometimes the message changes also. Depending on new experiences and new opportunities that unleash possibilities that weren't originally an option, you have to adapt.

One way to know when adjustments are needed is to periodically do assessments of what was and what is. For example, in my marriage, from time to time, my wife and I will go on more frequent dates. During these seasons, we explore each other's lives again and discuss who we've become. As a result, we've learned that one of the most lethal toxins to our relationship is predictability. Keeping our life together fresh means not taking each other for granted or assuming what used to bring each other joy is still the same. Open-mindedness, giving each other the right to grow and change, helps us not to grow apart as we age and evolve.

Relearning what you thought you knew well is important in every facet of life. Anytime you assess someone by who that person was without considering who she or he has become, you are setting yourself up for failure. People change. They evolve. Everyone grows and develops. We all want to be used at our highest capacity. Stability and security are important, but not at the expense of vibrancy and volatility.

I hate to hear someone say, "I knew you when…," as if this means that it's wrong for me to change. Everything matures. Anything that doesn't change is fruit dying on the vine! People are happiest when they can be appreciated for who they are and not just for who they were when you first met them. Our ability to grow and change, to learn and expand, keeps us curious, charismatic, exciting, and fresh!

Like so many aspects of life, this ability to adapt and grow requires you to be instinctive and not just informational. Information is based on past assessments, but instincts signal that something has changed. People often transform right in front of us, but we miss it because we're relying on old information or our first impression of them.

It's as useless as last year's newspaper to rely on what you used to know about a person. People need to be appreciated for who they are now. This is especially true when they are constantly improving themselves but imprisoned by your limited view of who they once were. Be sensitive to changes in those around you; pay attention to people. Looking at a person is far different from just seeing them. Alertness can stop you from longing for something that is accessible to you but not detected by you! I've been there.

Personal growth in others should be welcomed, even if it stretches us to grow ourselves. The Apostle Paul says that we act a certain way as babies, but when we grow, there should be a noticeable difference. When we have matured, evidence should show we are in a different phase.

❂ ❂ ❂ ❂

Prayer
Awesome God, I affirm that people change and commit myself to always be an observant student of the people with whom I'm in relationship. Give me the will to evaluate when a method needs to be changed and the courage to act upon my observations.
In Jesus' name. Amen.

25

FIGHT EXTINCTION

And now, Israel, what does the LORD your God require
of you, but to fear the LORD your God, to walk in all His
ways and to love Him, to serve the LORD your God with
all your heart and with all your soul, and to keep the
commandments of the LORD and His statutes which I
command you today for your good? Indeed heaven and
the highest heavens belong to the LORD your God, also the
earth with all that is in it. The LORD delighted only in your
fathers, to love them; and He chose their descendants after
them, you above all peoples, as it is this day. Therefore
circumcise the foreskin of your heart, and be stiff-necked no
longer.

Deuteronomy 10:12-16, NKJV

One of the most fascinating stories I've learned
about has to do with a dinosaur, an entire species
that reduced its own life span prematurely. An ar-
cheologist team researched the Apatosaurus, also known
as the brontosaurus, and how it became extinct. The Apa-

tosaurus was one of the tallest dinosaurs. It could stand on its hind legs and reach up to the top of the trees. So this is how the Apatosaurus was used to eating—standing tall and grazing the foliage at the very top of the tallest trees. But as the Apatosaurus continued to eat from the top, the growth of the trees didn't keep up with the demand. There were more Apatosaurus than the top leaves on the branches could feed. The trees didn't grow as fast as the Apatosaurus's appetite. So the Apatosaurus ran out of food to eat and eventually became extinct.

But upon further speculation about what happened, archeologists believe this dinosaur self-destructed. Other species died off because of climate change and predators, but the Apatosaurus died because it didn't take advantage of the other foliage available to it on lower tree branches. The Apatosaurus kept looking for food at the tip top of the trees. The animals didn't bend their necks. Had they, they would have found a new food supply; all of the food they'd need was right below their necks in the middle of the trees or on bushes. They epitomized stiff-necked. They were inflexible. They could not adjust to find anything else to eat even though vegetation was all around.

If you or your team cannot adjust your necks to see the possibilities around you, you are in danger of becoming extinct. If you and your team *can* adjust your views and see the potential around you, you can not only survive, you can grow and you can thrive and share your gifts.

Oftentimes, it takes a new crew to come in and see the possibilities. This is what happens in second marriages, new managements in old businesses, new leadership in churches, staff changes at a school. It can be tragic when someone else with less rigidity can turn your wilderness into vegetable garden by implementing simple things that were within your view, but you didn't bend your neck to see them.

Have you surrounded yourself with people who can bend and flex when needed? Are you open to hear what team members observe and see? Unorthodox thinkers are creative. They deviate from the traditional to the trans-formative. They break into new foliage. They discern the times and change to make things better.

Stiff-necked is what God called the Israelites through-out the Old Testament. And in today's verse, God speaks through Moses and instructs the people to stop being so stubborn. Are you stubborn? Are you set in a certain mode? Are you always predictable? Do you refuse to ad-just your view to see what other possibilities are open to you? Stiff-necked people will destroy vital opportunities because they can't adapt to trends and changes around them.

If you are stiff-necked, cleanse your heart and get in tune with your instincts. They could be telling you to look around and open up to new possibilities in ministry, in your marriage, in work. Adjusting your neck can help you fight extinction and remain relevant and in tune with needs.

Don't become like the Apatosaurus and die prematurely. You can fight extinction.

Prayer
Merciful Lord, forgive me when I refuse to look around and see new possibilities. Cleanse my heart and my thoughts to stay in tune with you and where you direct me. Thank you.
In Jesus' name. Amen.

26

SLOW DOWN AND FOCUS

*"Be still, and know that I am God! I will be honored by
every nation. I will be honored throughout the world."*
Psalm 46:10, NLT

In your quest to live a fulfilling, instinct-driven life,
it's important to understand that being busy doesn't
equate to being productive. Instinct followers realize
that they cannot do everything and need to spend their
time wisely, not busily.

When you are busy just doing, you do not have time to
listen and act on instincts. You get tied up in doing the
work, not in thinking about the possibilities or evaluating
the needs. You are just busy.

Some studies show that we spend 80 percent of the day
doing tasks that are mundane and ordinary. We spend
only about 20 percent of each day at our highest and best,
doing what we were created to do and in the area where
we can have the most impact.

What would happen if we turned that around? Some tasks need to be done even if they are not the most productive or don't need our best energy: check the email, return a call, etc. But imagine how energized and truly productive you'd be if you spent more time on the things that give you fulfillment, the things you were uniquely wired to do, and the things you bring the most value to. Imagine how well you would be able to listen to your instincts if you were able to do what naturally invigorates you.

Scripture even gives value to the importance of taking time to stop being busy and focus on what's really important. Psalm 46:10 reminds us to "Be still and know that I am God." This is a call to stop, to rest and be still, to focus on our Creator, and intimately know God, who can inspire us and invigorate us. When we are invigorated and focused, we are in the perfect position to hear our instincts, the inner urgings of our heart.

Being still may not seem like productive work, but it can yield more results than being busy. Not all people who have full schedules are productive. Even relationships can benefit from the beauty of stillness, the beauty of sitting and resting and being still. Not all marriages that are busy are healthy. Sit and be still to be invigorated to pursue what matters most.

❀ ❀ ❀ ❀

Dear Lord, slow me down. I sit here now, still, knowing you in this moment. I know that you are God, creator

of every good and perfect gift. I know that you are God, provider of all the strength and resources I need. I tune in to my inner instincts right now to prepare to do the most productive work.

In Jesus' name. Amen.

27

MANAGE TIME

*But I discipline my body and keep it under control, lest after
preaching to others I myself should be disqualified.*
1 Corinthians 9:27, ESV

In *Instinct*, I share that gamekeepers and wildlife spe-
cialists must burn off excess brush in order to maintain the ecological equilibrium. If this were not done,
the land would become overgrown, resulting in the excess
of some plants and animals and the extinction of others.
Farmers often use a similar technique to conduct a "controlled burn" on some of their fields. Burning off old crops
often adds nitrogen-rich nutrients to the soil and makes it
even more fertile for the next planting season.

Burning off the excess takes skill. The fire has to be intentionally lit and carefully monitored and contained.
These burn-offs also help prevent wildfires, since a light-
ning strike cannot set ablaze an area that has already been
scorched and scoured by flames. My guide told me that, as

odd as it sounds, in this way they use fire to stop fire.

Similarly, we must use directed effort to control misdi-rected effort. If you're consumed by busyness at the ex-pense of real business, perhaps you should set a new and different kind of fire. When you burn off the clutter of busyness and leave yourself time to think and study, you may get less done; but the things you do will be far more productive and ultimately more organic to what you are passionate about accomplishing. Your slow burn will yield more fruit and a better crop.

The fringe benefit of burning off the brush is a much clearer view of the terrain ahead. No one can see beyond their sight lines. And when cluttered with obstructions, our vision will always be impaired. It will take discipline to burn your fields, but we know there is much benefit in discipline.

Call on your instinctive imagination to answer a few questions. If you have a trusted friend, advisor, or part-ner, consider asking for help in answering these reflective questions:

Where do I need to clear a path so that I have room to maneuver toward my ultimate destination?

What needs to be burned away in order to refine my focus?

How can I unblock my view of who I am, what I could be, and where I could go?

My friend, if you decide to take control of your life and subdue the earth you have been given, then burn off the clutter of your life. Once you can see the ground beneath your feet again and the skyline above your head, launch yourself into your destiny. Look out for your bumper crops!

❂ ❂ ❂ ❂

Prayer
God, my Teacher and Leader, thank you for the lessons
I learn from nature and the process of caring for your
creation. Show me how to assess my life, burn off what
does not need to be, and focus more clearly on you as
you supply my needs.
Amen.

28

SURVEY THE LAND

"Is there anyone here who, planning to build a new house, doesn't first sit down and figure the cost so you'll know if you can complete it? If you only get the foundation laid and then run out of money, you're going to look pretty foolish. Everyone passing by will poke fun at you: 'He started something he couldn't finish.'

"Or can you imagine a king going into battle against another king without first deciding whether it is possible with his ten thousand troops to face the twenty thousand troops of the other? And if he decides he can't, won't he send an emissary and work out a truce?"
Luke 14:28-32, MSG

If you are following your instincts, there will no doubt come a time when you will have to cross boundaries. You will have to partner with someone who can take you to the next level, try a different technique, learn to use a new tool in your relationship, or otherwise spread your wings to cross your existing boundaries.

Scripture says you would be foolish to start something you couldn't finish. The same is true for crossing boundaries, even those led by instincts. You have to plan first.

When a question arises about land boundaries, you have a survey done. The survey can tell you who owns what part of the land and who is responsible for the various expenses such as taxation and maintenance. You wouldn't just buy a property and assume the seller knew exactly where the boundaries were. The survey specifies the boundaries and helps you determine whether you want to buy the land.

Ironically, time and time again, people walk into new situations or pursue new relationships without taking surveys. They have not considered the implications of their new beginning nor have they taken the time to consider the cost.

To not prepare for new territory is disrespectful to the opportunity. And if we believe that all good things are gifts from the Lord—aren't we in essence dissing God when we don't plan, assess the costs, do our homework? When we find ourselves wrapped up in the busyness of life, we can easily forsake the important step of assessing and surveying. If we are to be good stewards of all of the instinctive possibilities, we'll have to learn to survey the land.

How does it look to survey the land when it comes to opportunities? You consider the good and the bad, the pros and the cons. Are there red flags or warning signs that you need to be aware of? These signs don't always mean you should stop; they might just mean you should proceed as if the light were yellow, adding a few more stop gaps to assess things.

If you're looking to broaden your territory, assessing and surveying is a step you can't skip. You don't want to be left building a house that you can never move into because you didn't consider the cost before you laid the foundation. Cross boundaries—yes; slow down, survey the cost, pray for direction, and assess the situation—absolutely!

Prayer
All-Knowing and Wise God, teach me to slow down and consider the costs when pursuing new opportunities, places, and relationships. I will rely on you to help me make the best choices.
Amen.

29

RITUALS AND ROUTINES

Observe people who are good at their work—skilled work-
ers are always in demand and admired; they don't take a
backseat to anyone.

Proverbs 22:29, MSG

We have to be careful of rituals and routines; they can be dream killers and deafen our natural instincts. The world is unfortunately filled with people who are not in touch with their instincts and are stuck doing tasks, following routines, and performing rituals that have little or no meaning to their core purpose. Frustrated and hopeless, multitudes complain about going to work, not because they are lazy, but because they are unchallenged, unfilled.

Anything we do for years—day in and day out—that doesn't match the inner imprint of our gifting will eventually become monotonous and routine, ritualistic and frustrating. Think of it like a key; it may fit in a lock, but it won't necessarily open the door. You can do the job, but it isn't quite what you're wired to do; so you never unlock the amazing possibilities that come from operating in your gifts, following your passions, and listening to your instincts.

If you find the link between the external career and the internal call, you can tap into the instincts. But to do this, you have to navigate through the maze of low-hanging opportunities and seek the open door that awaits you.

When you have the vision and instincts to see what is invisible behind the door of routines, you can open it and step into your destiny.

Great instincts lead to great promotion. So, even in the midst of routine, you can look for the things that invigorate you. You can consider your patchwork created by God and focus on what makes you tick. If you're fortunate, you can utilize this gifting in your current work place. And the more you follow your gifts, the more room they will make for you (Proverbs 18:16). Your gifts will create positions and possibilities you didn't know existed. Excellent workers are those who are following their gifting; new jobs are created for them. Scripture says because of their skills, these people "don't take a back seat to anyone."

Now, if you don't think your current work place provides room for you to exercise your gifts, consider your hobbies, your side jobs, and what you do when you're not punching the clock. Doing these things—even if on the side—can help you find energy that will make the routine, mundane tasks seem less mundane. You will gain energy and insight you didn't know was possible...and soon, you'll be doing the routines with more purpose. The rituals will take on new meaning. You will have a renewed sense of who you were created to be so you will see even the 9-to-5 (or whatever hours you might work) differently. You might just become a problem solver, learning ways to create new solutions. And we all know leaders are solution-oriented and valuable to any organization or relationship they are a part of.

How do you feel about your day-to-day activities? The ministries you are involved with? The relationships you hold important? Are you going about doing the same old same old? Try bringing a fresh perspective fueled by your instincts and watch things change. Watch your skills improve and your demand increase. You will be fulfilled and others will be blessed. It's a win-win situation.

Prayer
Lord, thank you for another chance to see my work, my relationships, my ministry in a new way as I work unto you. I forgo the mundane and usual and seek the new and fresh solutions.
In your name and power. Amen.

30

ACKNOWLEDGE GOD

Trust in the Lord with all your heart, and do not rely on your own insight. In all your ways acknowledge him, and he will make straight your paths.
Proverbs 3:5-6, NRSV

There's a vital point to fully understand when you are discovering how to live instinctively: when you fully connect to your passions and live in balance with intellect and instincts, you know you haven't done anything alone. You have to acknowledge God, our Creator. Instinct followers understand their gifts—and their very being—as coming directly from God. They see their instincts as the personal handiwork God has placed inside of them. They recognize that while instinctive, heart-felt living pulls from the center, it does not rely solely on our own insight. It connects to God and relies on God's Spirit. Instinct followers will not arrogantly think they have made it on their own; they will always acknowledge God and will continue to seek God's guidance.

Acknowledging God can do powerful things in your life. It makes you humbly point back to the Gift Giver. So when you prosper and grow and expand, people see God's handiwork. When you acknowledge the Creator as your designer and your gift giver, you are saying thank you. When you help people based on your God-given talents, you acknowledge the One who made you—the One in whom you move and have your very being (Acts 17:28).

As you journey on this path of living by instinct, don't ever forget to acknowledge God, your Creator. And I'm not talking about through mere words—like you're receiving a Grammy and giving God a shout-out. Your entire being should show that you thank God. How you relate to people should show that you thank God. The new opportunities you share should show you acknowledge God. The instincts you follow point you back to your ultimate trust and faith in God.

Your prayer life, your worship life, your entire life should reflect who is in the driver's seat directing you and helping you to live according to your instinct. How is your prayer life? How much time do you spend talking to God? How much time do you spend acknowledging all that God has done and is doing in your life? How do you show others you rely on God for guidance?

Take heart, my friend. You're not alone trying to find your inner urges. You have someone far greater than you and working on your behalf. Just remember to tap into that wealth of resource and give God the glory and the thanks. That's true acknowledgment.

✿ ✿ ✿ ✿

Prayer
Almighty God, I acknowledge you as my Lord, Creator, and Savior. I am so thankful and grateful to you for all of your gifts. I commit myself to trust you with everything and humbly give you all the glory.
In Jesus' name. Amen.

31

YOUR NETWORK

*So in Christ we, though many, form one body, and each
member belongs to all the others. We have different gifts,
according to the grace given to each of us. If your gift is
prophesying, then prophesy in accordance with your faith; if
it is serving, then serve; if it is teaching, then teach.*
Romans 12:5-7, NIV

Living successfully by instinct will require a variety
of complementary skills and talents; and they will
all need to work together in harmony to achieve results beyond what you could have achieved by yourself or
by sheer talent. If you're not comfortable with the concept
of networking—or working with others—you will need to
learn to become comfortable.

Networking is a vital part of successful people's lives.
These people know they are not masters at everything.
They know they are not lone rangers. What they need is
a team of people surrounding them with complementary
skills. Living by instinct—by its very nature—makes you

extend beyond your coworkers, employees, and casual acquaintances. Those following their instincts encounter people from a wide spectrum of professional and personal endeavors. The most successful people have a large network.

Consider the word *network*. It really underlines the fact that nets are woven together from strings going in different directions that connect at a certain point. The more strings that are working together, the larger the net; and the larger the net, the bigger the catch.

So get out of your comfort zone and enjoy networking. Don't be afraid to meet people who do not look and act like you, who have different backgrounds, and who do different things. Difference is great. Networks are based on strands that cross lines and make connections in spite of facing different directions or diverse perspectives.

Think of what Paul wrote to the Romans. We need all gifts to operate and form one body. Each gift does something different—and it should do it according to the measure of faith. Together, prophesying, serving, and teaching work to form the body of Christ and carry out the necessary work. One gift won't cut it; alone, it can't do it. The church needs a variety of gifts operating together.

Jesus recognized the effectiveness of fishermen using nets; there's benefit in working with a net that a single line can never touch. Potential effectiveness increases by diverse associations. Connect the dots and let your network work for you.

Prayer
My God and Lord, thank you for the variety of gifts you
have given your people. I see the benefit in networking
and connecting with those who may be different than
I am, and with your help I will break barriers to live
instinctively.
In Jesus' name. Amen.

32

THE HEART OF THE MATTER

My son, pay attention to what I say; turn your ear to my words. Do not let them out of your sight, keep them within your heart; for they are life to those who find them and health to one's whole body. Above all else, guard your heart, for everything you do flows from it.
Proverbs 4:20-23, NIV

Instincts come from inside. Instincts are your inner inclinations. Therefore, your heart is very important. Out of the heart, not out of the head, flows the issues of life. We are limited when we operate only from the intellectual and psychological; we are limited when we refuse to pay attention to the spiritual inclinations residing in us.

The mind may guide you in what you do—and that's great—but the heart affirms your passion to do it. And ultimately, this is what will move you.

Within your passions lie the clues to your deeper purpose—what you were designed and deposited on earth to do. We need to put our ears to our hearts and listen to our inner workings to catch the beat so we can be in tuned with what we are created to be.

Finding people who are in sync with our beat can form a more perfect union—a union that allows us to do what we were created to do, find the people we were meant to affect, and provide the power that comes from alignment with purpose.

What's in your heart? What makes your heart skip a beat? Pay attention to your heart. Scripture reminds us to guard it—to take special care of what goes into it, what colors it, and what comes close to it. Our heart is so precious that we need to protect it; after all, it houses the secret formula for our passions, for us to follow our instincts. Protecting our heart also means to pay special attention to what we are exposed to. If we feed our core with God's promises, affirmations, and positive reminders, we will have a more healthy heart that is ready and prepared to lead us—if we will listen.

Listening to your heart means listening beyond information. It means no longer being confined to where you are and experiencing the freedom to discover where you were meant to be. If we will listen to its drumbeat, if we have the courage to be wooed by our heart's wisdom, then we will find our answer. We could spend the rest of our lives in a rhythm so in sync with our heart that the melody transforms all areas of our lives into an integrated harmonic symphony of satisfaction.

✿ ✿ ✿ ✿

Prayer
God Almighty, as I listen to the beat of my heart, I know
you created me for a purpose. I desire to follow your purpose for my life. Show me how to pay attention to what
flows from my heart to find my passion.
In Jesus' name. Amen.

33

COMMON DENOMINATORS

A gift opens the way and ushers the giver into the presence of the great.

Proverbs 18:16, NIV

As you begin to think more about living by instinct, you may wonder how life will change and how you will be able to do all that is set before you. I am a testimony that your gifts will open new doors and new opportunities. And you will be able to handle the ones you are supposed to touch.

It's like a juggler handling two or more balls. If he has just one ball in the air, it's not juggling; he's simply tossing a ball. But when the juggler begins to juggle, he starts with two balls in the air. He practices throwing them up and catching them at different times and in a special rhythm that helps him know when to throw one and catch the other. Then, when he has mastered juggling two balls, he progresses to three; and the really good jugglers move to four or more balls, which are all thrown and caught in a special rhythm that allows the juggler to touch them all without letting any fall to the floor.

Instinct followers are jugglers. All their balls are in some way connected.

I have film production. I have writing. I speak at college campuses and various leadership conferences. I have church ministry and a pastoral team that I enjoy leading. I preach, which is my calling and my heart. I also have a music label, and I occasionally produce plays. There's no way I could juggle all of these responsibilities unless I truly understood their common denominator—communication, especially to people who need to tap into their God-given power and move forward.

If you find your common denominators, you can juggle everything and manage to get your hands on all the balls and find the right rhythm to keep them moving. Instinctive leaders know how to keep them all in the air at just the right rhythm without dropping the balls on the ground.

The same kind of rhythm is seen when a cook prepares a dinner. The cook preheats the oven, prepares the marinade, and keeps the potatoes soaking while the roast is in the oven. They set the table while the soup simmers. Their pacing is everything. They have to find the rhythm to make things work together at the right time.

If you have the kind of personality, product, or mission that excels—especially through following your instincts— you will inevitably find yourself operating in different arenas at the same time. The Bible describes it as a man's gift making room for him. Following your instincts and applying your intellect will bring you success; it will open new doorways of destiny and new windows of worldwide wonder.

Get ready to connect to your mission and juggle, my friend.

✪ ✪ ✪ ✪

Prayer
Precious Lord, thank you for the new opportunities that
are opening because I'm learning to follow instincts.
Show me how to use these gifts to bless you and others.
Thank you for opportunities.
Amen.

34

INTEGRATION IS KEY

But in fact God has placed the parts in the body, every one of them, just as he wanted them to be. If they were all one part, where would the body be? As it is, there are many parts, but one body. The eye cannot say to the hand, "I don't need you!" And the head cannot say to the feet, "I don't need you!"

1 Corinthians 12:18-21, NIV

In *Instinct*, I share tools intuitive leaders need to sharpen to navigate new areas that become available to them. One of those vital principles is what I call integration. Successful leaders learn how to integrate, rather than simply tolerate or accept differences. Whether in business, marriage, or other areas of life, alliances work only when the needs of both parties are met and respected. We want to pursue a cross-section of opportunity, an integration of expectations.

In this pursuit, the art of negotiation becomes an essential tool. Those who negotiate from a selfish perspective of getting what they want at any cost, without respecting others' needs, will ultimately fail. An integrated strategy inherently addresses each individual's motives, agendas, and goals in the midst of a larger, shared goal. This integration-based strategy includes the fulfillment of those needs in such a way that all differences are respected without losing sight of the ultimate objective.

It is similar to what Scripture says about the parts of the body. A hand has a different job than the foot; they are not the same. They don't look alike; they are located in separate areas of the body, and they have distinct functions. You'll have trouble if you ask the foot to act just like the hand and vice versa. In order for the human body—and even the body of Christ—to operate, each member needs to be respected for its unique abilities. Each member needs to be appreciated for what it can do and allowed to perform as it was designed.

You don't have to give up your gifts, but do appreciate those who have different gifts than yours and integrate them into your life.

There is a crucial difference between merely tolerating differences and integrating them. The term *tolerance* is deeply overrated. Tolerating differences might be a politically correct expression; but in order for people to feel fulfilled in life, they must be much more than tolerated. They must feel that their talents, resources, and needs are an integral part of a successful whole. No one feels comfortable when they're merely tolerated. And toleration tends to be a temporary token. Most people can be tolerant for only so long before their patience wears thin and shreds the garment of acceptance they gave to others.

If you want to be successful, you must negotiate by respecting differences, accommodating them, and even valuing them so that people feel that their uniqueness isn't just tolerated but is celebrated and integrated into the plan. An integration of participants' needs and desires must be an integral part of any union in order for it to succeed. This is true for everyone, including me. Without integrating what you know to be my needs as a spouse, a partner, a customer, an employee, or colleague ultimately dooms our relationship. If you're going to broaden your circle, you must change your thinking to integrate the other individual, auxiliary, or company's objectives with your own. Without this component, others will only feel violated by the association, and the opportunity will eventually dissolve.

How well do you accept and integrate differences? Does everyone need to agree with you or make you feel comfortable culturally in order to work with you?

Don't put up roadblocks on your path to instinctive living. Open up and accept the variety of gifts available to you through others who do not look, think, or act like you. How much you will get done might surprise you.

❄ ❄ ❄ ❄

Prayer

Creator of a masterfully diverse universe, thank you for creating the body to reflect how we should work together. Thank you for each gift that helps to glorify you and lead us instinctively. Recreate in me love for each person you place in my path to instinctive living, and teach me to value their gifts and contribution.

In Jesus' name. Amen.

35

WHAT'S STOPPING YOU?

The LORD God took the man and put him in the Garden of Eden to work it and take care of it. And the LORD God commanded the man, "You are free to eat from any tree in the garden; but you must not eat from the tree of the knowledge of good and evil, for when you eat from it you will certainly die." The LORD God said, "It is not good for the man to be alone. I will make a helper suitable for him."
Genesis 2:15-18, NIV

Another important lesson instinctive followers need to learn is to surmount roadblocks—those we impose on ourselves and those set by society. Our instincts remind us that we are social creatures and we are meant to be in relationship with each other. Think of Adam and Eve. God created the first pair and put us humans in relationship for our own fulfillment as well as for the enhancement of our ever-expanding community. God did not intend for us to be alone. But God didn't make Adam and Eve exactly alike—and thank God for the beautiful differences in man and woman!

But instead of maximizing our God-given need and tendency to bond, we often build social constructs that fence us in and limit us. We follow what society would have us to do, or what our particular culture or our families think is normative. We create visible and intangible barriers around ourselves; we invent prisons both literal and figurative! We build fences and barriers, restrictions and walls, and ultimately feel lonely or muddle through life in mediocre relationships.

Like lions of the field and eagles of the air, we were born to live free. Our ultimate human instinct is always freedom—freedom of thought, freedom of passion, and freedom of purpose. You'll never fulfill your destiny until you break out of the social constructs that define and limit what is within you!

What social fences have you erected to keep you with the same people who think and dress like you, who have the same goals? Jump your fence; walk across the street. You may meet someone who can inspire you and motivate you to follow your instincts. You in turn may do the same for them.

Don't worry about your differences. Consider your differences as a gift from God to reproduce ideas, thoughts, and new possibilities. Adam and Eve working together produced descendants. Work together while being true to yourself and God. It's what you were created for.

✿ ✿ ✿ ✿

Prayer

God of creation, thank you for creating me and giving me an instinct to be free. I will break free of the constructs that hinder me from truly living as you have designed me.

In Jesus' name. Amen.

36

INSPIRATION, A TOOL TO MOVE BEYOND BARRIERS

Those who live at the ends of the earth stand in awe of your wonders. From where the sun rises to where it sets, you inspire shouts of joy.
Psalm 65:8, NLT

Four principles or tools can assist us in breaking down the walls that keep us in our own self-imposed boundaries. One of those tools is inspiration, something inside us that instinctively pushes us beyond those around us. It may be why you don't fit. People who are meant to lead have trouble being satisfied with those who seek the normal and are satisfied with the status quo. Their inspiration instinctively takes them beyond barriers and leads them to color outside the lines.

Inspiration springs from an instinct, an internal compass that points across familiar lines toward the unknown. Like a spark kindling tinder into a flame, inspiration ignites you to act on what you envision in your imagination. Others may encounter the same external stimuli but fail to have it inspire them with new ideas or innovative approaches. Those who balance their intellects with instinct know that inspiration is often their offspring.

Just observing God's creation inspires shouts of joy. When we sit back and get in tune with how God has wired us and our inner leanings, we can know our inspiration. We can find out what inspires us.

Your mind takes in data, performs due diligence, processes information—that's intellect. But your instinct converts knowledge to power. Your instinctive deductive reasoning becomes inspired. It guides your quest to move beyond the scope of ordinary accomplishments and requires you to blaze trails and knock down walls and barriers—that's inspiration!

Inspiration is such a powerful tool and, in part, explains the way our intelligence complements our instincts. We take in information as raw material, as fuel, and then our instincts shape it into the best form for our current needs. This ability to adapt what we know externally with what we know internally yields inspiration, which bridges the two.

Whether we call it a hunch, an intuition, or a crazy idea, inspiration creates a fire that can provide heat, warmth, and energy to a situation that otherwise remains cold and flat.

What inspires you? Think about what you gravitate toward when given time to relax and recharge. Are you always watching cooking shows on the Food Network, tinkering with recipes to make them your own? Maybe you're exploring new apps, thinking about the ones you wish existed that you can't find. Do you find yourself perusing history books and travel brochures about a foreign land or culture that captivates you? Are you drawn to the latest leadership training course that's coming to town?

Pay attention to what nourishes and stimulates your heart, soul, and imagination for clues to what inspires you. Make note of inspiring moments. Developing your awareness can lead you to listen more intentionally to your instincts. Listening to your instincts jump-starts the process of creating your destiny.

Prayer
Wonderful God, bring back to my memory what inspires me. I will use my God-given inspiration to live a more fulfilling life—to bring glory to you and blessing to your people.
In Jesus' name. Amen.

37

INSTINCTS IN ACTION

*What good is it, my brothers and sisters, if someone claims
to have faith but has no deeds? Can such faith save them?
Suppose a brother or a sister is without clothes and daily
food. If one of you says to them, "Go in peace; keep warm
and well fed," but does nothing about their physical needs,
what good is it? In the same way, faith by itself, if it is not
accompanied by action, is dead.*
James 2:14-17, NIV

Perhaps the most vital step in the principles used to
cross boundaries is execution. A net doesn't work
until it's thrown. No fisherman would make a net
for fishing and leave it on the boat. Execution is critical for
accomplishment. If you don't execute the plans you have
in place, it doesn't matter how inspired you may be. Inspiration without execution will always lead to frustration.

It's the same as having a whole lot of faith—knowing all
about God and all that God can do—but not doing anything with it. Faith requires action. If you believe God is

a provider, you know you need to go out and gather what God has provided. You know you need to go out and put into action what you have faith to receive. It's all words if you don't act upon it. It's as sad as someone telling a homeless person to keep warm without giving that person a coat or a place to stay. Faith and actions work together, just like our instincts and our networks. While we make plans, we must take steps to see it done—to the end.

Whenever I look beyond my line of achievement, I know I must build a bridge that takes me there. If I build a promising relationship, proposal, or team but fail to execute, it won't be long before I've lost my opportunity. If I can't transform ideas into actions, my ideas become worthless.

I can't tell you how many times I've been in a meeting or with a group of bright, creative, talented people who get stuck in their own ideas. Their ideas are good, some even great, but without execution it's ultimately impossible to evaluate the worth of an idea. In order for your instinctive ability to produce a product, create a craft, or establish an industry, you must have action points.

Evaluate your history. If you are known for having great ideas but being unable to follow through or for overpromising and under-delivering, ask yourself what's stopping you from acting? You may need a push to put your faith into action. You may need a team that can take your ideas, form action items, and execute them. Don't let your great ideas get stuck in brainstorm mode. Seek help to get them to the implementation point.

Your ability to transform inspiration into reality is only as powerful as your execution. All of us have the ability to achieve more by harnessing our intellect to our instincts and then taking action. We often need other people. Collaborative efforts, we've seen, are usually the most effective, and it's an incredible breach of trust to other stakeholders when any individual does not do their part in the process. When everyone does their part, they achieve the large-scale results that benefit them all.

Be known as someone who not only follows your instincts for excellence but exchanges them for action and carries out decisions once you've made them. Eventually, your ability to execute will become a matter of integrity.

An instinct without execution is only a regret. Put your faith into action.

✿ ✿ ✿ ✿

Prayer
Glorious God, be with me as I honestly assess my life and tendencies. Forgive me for not always putting my faith in action to execute plans that need to happen and that will have an impact on others.
In Jesus' name. Amen.

BE READY FOR ADVERSITY

My dear brothers and sisters, take note of this: Everyone should be quick to listen, slow to speak and slow to become angry, because human anger does not produce the righteousness that God desires.

James 1:19-20, NIV

Following your instincts will lead you into new territories. You are dynamic and designed for change. When you are doing what you need to do, your territory will by definition grow. And there are some things you just have to be prepared for when you enter a new environment, when you expand, or when you leave behind the old cage.

One of the things I think people overlook when going forward is adversity. They forget—or refuse—to prepare for it. I know it may seem like a benign environment, but new is new and predators will be waiting. Sometimes the splendor, the challenge, and the brilliance of affirmation shine so brightly that those who are blessed to step into a new arena become dazzled by the opportunity and blinded to the adversity. No matter how friendly the welcome party seems, always know that the bobcats come out at night! Predators can be there, awaiting us.

Whenever you arrive on the shores of a new career, vocation, or aspiration, you always arrive as an immigrant. You have a different scent on you, and all the animals know it! No amount of kindness can alter the fact that the other animals in your new world feel threatened by your arrival—which means you must be prepared to do some sniffing as well! Instinctive leaders know this and act accordingly.

Only fools rush in where the brave dare not tread. And while it is a wonderful blessing to have the gate open to a fresh opportunity, it is naïve to think that you are walking into a sterile, unbiased environment. So sniff out your new world before you do too much barking. Knowing who's who will save you from ending up on the menu of some overly aggressive, attention-starved, attack-prone coyote who comes out only at night.

In new environments especially, learn to read the body language as well as the new words in the native tongue. You should be listening—at all times. And you can't listen when you are talking. So, as Scripture says, you should be slow to speak when you are the new kid on the block or are entering new territories. So much can be communicated that's contrary to what is actually being said. And you can't see this when your mouth is open. Instinctive leaders have learned the art of timing, patience, and are alert to their surroundings—when they are talking and especially when they are observing.

New dogs in the yard don't usually know the rules of engagement. It is most important that you do a lot of looking and sniffing before you do much barking. Others already know you are there. Proceed with caution without looking afraid. It should be instinctive to check out your new territory! It should be instinctive to listen and not always speak.

Prayer
Loving Lord, remind me to be slow to speak and quick to listen, especially when in new environments. Help me to be wise when entering new areas so I can instinctively learn the lay of the land and make the most of every God-given opportunity. Thank you.
In Jesus' name. Amen.

39

HANDLE THE CHALLENGE

*But we have this treasure in jars of clay to show that this
all-surpassing power is from God and not from us. We are
hard pressed on every side, but not crushed; perplexed, but
not in despair; persecuted, but not abandoned; struck down,
but not destroyed.*

2 Corinthians 4:7-9, NIV

While everyone who follows instincts isn't always a leader, most leaders—especially good and effective leaders—are in touch with their instincts and follow them regularly.

There are qualities instinctive leaders have in abundance that followers don't. One of those is how leaders handle challenges.

God promotes us to our level of tolerance for pain. So when you whine about how overwhelmed you are and how you're not able to inspire others, you're basically saying: Don't take me any higher. I can't handle anymore.

If you start pushing something that you can't carry, watch your muscles grow stronger and watch how people will come to your aid. Instinctive leadership never retreats from chaos, questions, unreasonable demands, and burdens.

The better you are at responding to a challenge, the more apt you are to succeed.

Take the attitude the Apostle Paul had when writing to the Corinthians. Paul knew he and his fellow Christians were weak, but Paul encouraged believers to look to God for true strength. The Almighty's strength in them was like a special treasure enclosed in unworthy, simple jars. And if you view yourself like this, you recognize that challenges don't have to crush you. They can work to make you stronger—to show the amazing power of God working within you. You can be confused, but not in despair. There is a difference. You might receive a blow, but it won't make you give up. And you know that you will never be left alone or destroyed, for truly Jesus' promise remains true—to be with you always (Matthew 28:20).

So think like an instinctive leader and remember that the demands of life don't matter nearly as much as your response to them. How will you respond to the challenge in your life right now? Will you merely acquiesce or avoid? Will you be crushed under the pressure, give up in despair, or withdraw? Or will you chart your course, organize your assets, and take on the challenge before you?

When opportunity calls, instinctive leaders answer. In Jesus' mighty power, you can press forward and make God's strength even more evident.

Prayer
Dear God, I need you to show me how to see challenges and obstacles as a way for your mighty power to be seen more clearly. I want to see trials as a way to build strength and rely on you more fully. Forgive me for complaining; help me instead to see the possibilities. You are my amazing Teacher and I am forever grateful!
In Jesus' name. Amen.

40

DIFFERENT STYLES

Watch what God does, and then you do it, like children who learn proper behavior from their parents. Mostly what God does is love you. Keep company with him and learn a life of love. Observe how Christ loved us. His love was not cautious but extravagant. He didn't love in order to get something from us but to give everything of himself to us. Love like that.

Ephesians 5:1-2, MSG

If you want to be successful in any endeavor as a leader, you will seek to understand others. You will nurture relationships, always observing and learning about your partners so you can understand them better and better. It's hard to truly lead someone that you don't understand.

Leadership isn't a one-size-fits-all endeavor. Those who only have one propensity will not be able to handle all issues or work well with all types of people. An effective leader seeks to understand what works best in each situation. These leaders put their team members' needs at the center of their operation. Like Christ, they care more about people than anything else.

Our personalities, professional abilities, and social skills all contribute to our leadership styles, but instincts also inform the way we lead. Leaders can be characterized by the way they handle conflict, make decisions, and prioritize needs. When you know your leadership style and the people you lead, you know when you need to make adjustments. It's not being fickle; it's dealing in understanding.

People of different temperaments respond to different leadership styles and approaches. The most effective leader understands this and studies the best approach to get the results needed from each individual. Strong, effective leaders share some qualities from all leadership styles. They know they can't simply be one-dimensional. They adapt to the prerequisites of any given situation.

Having a strong sense of everyone's strengths and weaknesses will help you to determine best-case scenarios, similar to the way a carpenter chooses a tool for the job he's presently tackling. It doesn't mean the hammer is always the best tool—but you better believe any carpenter worth his weight has a good, sturdy hammer in the tool kit. The same holds true for screwdrivers. You don't use a screwdriver for every task; but ask any carpenter about a screwdriver, and he or she should show you a wide array of choices—all tucked away in his or her tool box—ready to be used when the job calls for it.

Instinctive leaders learn to relate to people according to

their needs. They know the importance of dwelling with others according to the knowledge they've gleaned from being instinctive observers, and the results they get delineate the difference between leaders and followers.

Prayer
All-Knowing and All-Powerful God, thank you for the gift to understand people. I vow to use the tools available to me to deal with those I am blessed to be in relationship with according to an instinctive understanding.
In Jesus' name. Amen.

LEAVING THE CAGE

But the fruit of the Spirit is love, joy, peace, forbearance,
kindness, goodness, faithfulness, gentleness and self-control.
Galatians 5:22-23a, NIV

We all have cages of comfort. Our cages protect us, but they also isolate us—not only from what lies outside, but also from discovering what lies within us. Before we decide to leave a cage, there are some important considerations.

Much like a lion who is reintroduced into the wild, we have to free ourselves from the habits of captivity. For example, the idea of freeing yourself from a dead-end job seems liberating and purchasing your own home is a dream, but while the cage may be confining, freedom also comes at a cost. Although many of us aren't happy in the cages and feel drawn to the wild, we must never underestimate the fierceness of freedom and the danger of the new world of self-fulfillment.

Ask any entrepreneur who has struck out on his own and he will tell you that he works more hours than he did at that dead-end job. The entrepreneur doesn't just work from 9-5; she doesn't stop working. When everyone has gone home for the day, the visionary is usually still thinking of the next step or how to improve the processes. He's out networking, reading about the next technologies, scoping out new trends. The new wild has more freedom but also has more responsibilities.

Leaving the cage will require new skills and a metamorphosis.

It's no wonder one aspect of the fruit of the Spirit—the characteristics that are exemplified when we are living according to the Holy Spirit—is self-control or discipline. Spirit followers rely on God to help them control their mouth and habits. Likewise, those who leave the cage will also need to control habits to ensure success. It's not just about freedom. You will have to go out and catch your meal instead of being fed in the cage. You will have to have mentors and tutors to help you learn the new habitat when you follow your instincts. For the homeowner, you will have to budget for home repairs versus relying on your landlord to handle them. For the fulfilling relationship, you will need to think about another's needs, not just your own.

God's Spirit is a great guide to consistently prompt you and direct your path—if you pay attention. Don't despise self-control and discipline as you step out into the wild.

Stay connected to God with all of your being so that you know when God's Spirit is leading you to follow your instinct.

Prayer
Dear God, I want to learn to use the tools you have given me to transition from my cage to new territory. Thank you for equipping me with all I need.
In Jesus' name. Amen.

42

I WANT TO KNOW MYSELF

You made all the delicate, inner parts of my body and knit me together in my mother's womb. Thank you for making me so wonderfully complex! Your workmanship is marvelous—how well I know it.

Psalm 139:13-14, NLT

When you are ready to activate your instinct, you should seek elements of excellence that inspire you. Spend time studying yourself. Reflect on what appeals to your heart and ignites something deep inside you—the articles that arrest your attention, the topics that tantalize your thoughts.

Learning about yourself doesn't require a battery of aptitude tests; you simply need to pay attention to yourself and your habits and the things that stir you—even the things no one else knows about you. What books are at your bedside? What pages do you check on Pinterest? What blogs do you read?

Think about your childhood. What are your favorite memories? What gave you pleasure? Was it building new, never-before-seen structures with Legos? Creating stories about your friends on another planet? Caring for your pets with love and attention? Whatever once had the power to float your boat can still rock your world.

Getting to know God better can give you more information. God is your Creator, the One who knit you together in your mother's womb. God knew you before you were able to breathe on your own. God knew you in that secret place hidden inside of your mother. God knows you better than anyone else.

What do you pray about? What do you talk to God about? What has God put inside of you that no one may know about. Remembering that God truly knows you can also give you comfort and faith that God can help you discover the paths you should venture down.

As you search for your passions, don't disregard any attraction, interest, or proclivity as being too "out there" to examine and extract information from. You never know what you might discover by thinking outside the boxes that culture, conformity, and critics have tried to impose.

When you have a list of those preferences, look for patterns and common denominators. What gets you going? What sparks a creative impulse? Who motivates you as a role model? Where do you feel most alive?

Don't limit yourself. You are the most fascinating person you will know! Allow the true you to come out. This is the soil where you will discover seeds planted long ago waiting to burst through the surface.

Prayer
Amazing Creator, I thank you for making me and knowing me. Allow me to tap into all that you've placed in my heart so that I may do what you've called me to do in this life.
In Jesus' name. Amen.

43

EXPOSURE TO GREATNESS

No one will be able to stand up against you all the days of your life. As I was with Moses, so I will be with you; I will never leave you nor forsake you.
Joshua 1:5, NIV

Instinct followers know that they need to be exposed to a variety of people in a variety of areas. We often learn more from our differences than our similarities, and those ascending the ladder of success can watch and learn from those a few rungs above them.

Hanging out with people who inspire you can give you great ideas and a glimpse into what it looks like to follow your instincts. While you won't be emulating these people, your exposure to them can fuel your self-discovery and energize your instincts.

Consider the fact that artists have natural talent but need instruction and inspiration in order to produce their own unique innovation. Their natural talent will only get them so far; they need the input of teachers, peers, and practitioners. When artists are exposed to great historical works, they gain a solid foundation that allows them to branch out into new areas of experimentation and hybridization. As a writer friend says: "You have to know the rules and the reasons behind them before you can break them!"

That's what Joshua did during his many years under Moses' tutelage. Watching Moses lead the people of Israel served as Joshua's training to lead their descendants once Moses died (see Joshua 1). And just as God had been with Moses, God promised to be with Joshua.

So while leading a nation could have felt like a daunting task, Joshua had been prepared and he had the promise that God would be with him. Following our instincts will feel lonely at times. It's not always popular to pursue what drives you. But when you're following your God-given instincts, God will be with you—just as the Almighty was with Moses and the great Jehovah was with Joshua. Remember God's promise to always be with you.

People who are comfortable in their cages will not always be happy that you have decided to flee the confines. They may feel threatened as you venture out on your own. They may criticize your passionate pursuits and seek to sabotage your date with destiny. But people who are instinctively led will encourage you to greatness. Birds of a feather flock together and often recognize each other. Instinct followers know the joy of living a fulfilled life and desire to see others in their zone, too. Happiness attracts happiness. Passion followers attract passion followers. Instinct lovers will attract instinct lovers.

Go out and be great!

Prayer

Dear Lord, I know that you are always with me. When life seems tough and following my instincts is hard, I will rely on your promise. Teach me to gain inspiration from others who are following their instincts.

In Jesus' name. Amen.

44

GET FREE

The Spirit of the Sovereign Lord is on me, because the Lord has anointed me to proclaim good news to the poor. He has sent me to bind up the brokenhearted, to proclaim freedom for the captives and release from darkness for the prisoners, to proclaim the year of the Lord's favor and the day of vengeance of our God, to comfort all who mourn, and provide for those who grieve in Zion.
Isaiah 61:1-3a, NIV

Following your instincts is also about freedom, liberating yourself to live as you were designed to live. Our ultimate instinct is always freedom—freedom of thought, freedom of passion, and freedom of purpose.

Belief in God can give us the faith to liberate our minds and others. Just as Isaiah proclaimed in today's Scripture and Jesus later fulfilled in Luke 4, we are given power to free captives. The term *captive* not only refers to those who are behind prison bars or held against their will; the mind is a power tool, and it too can be held captive. Allowing

God to help you follow your instincts can free your mind and bring liberation.

Think about how the mind works. What you allow to grow and fester in your mind will eventually influence how you act. This is something that slave holders understood all too well during America's dark history. These slave holders knew that the key to freedom was in the mind of the enslaved, which is why those in bondage were forbidden to learn to read. Once the person in bondage thought like a free person, they would be nearly impossible to control. If you liberate someone's thinking, it is only a matter of time before chains cannot hold them.

I listen to people because I can always gain some wisdom that will influence me. But when a person tries to force ideas upon me, the conversation is over. My mind cannot be controlled by another person's thinking.

You will need to adopt the same type of attitude if you truly want to live as you were meant to be—free. Sometimes you will have to act regardless of what others say. Sometimes you will have to go against the grain to pay attention to your instinct. Freedom has a cost, but being imprisoned has a greater price. Which one will you choose? How will you feed your mind so you can act freely?

Follow Isaiah and Christ and free yourself from the captivating thoughts set up to contain you. You, too, will find liberation.

✪ ✪ ✪ ✪

Prayer

God, my Liberator, I thank you for the power to free my mind from thoughts that might keep me captive. Thank you for freedom of thought and action. I ask you to guide me as I follow my instincts and tune out negativity. In Jesus' name. Amen.

45

POWERFUL COMBINATIONS

Jesus called his twelve disciples to him and gave them au-
thority to drive out impure spirits and to heal every disease
and sickness. These are the names of the twelve apostles:
first, Simon (who is called Peter) and his brother Andrew;
James son of Zebedee, and his brother John; Philip and Bar-
tholomew; Thomas and Matthew the tax collector; James
son of Alphaeus, and Thaddaeus; Simon the Zealot and
Judas Iscariot, who betrayed him.
Matthew 10:1-4, NIV

Jesus selected a diverse group of men to call his apostles. Read the list, study who they are, and you'll see
Jesus had a fiery, yet rock-like Peter. Jesus called the
sons of thunder, also known as James and John, who were
fishermen. He chose a tax collector, someone who was
scorned at the time. He even chose the man that he knew
would betray him—after all, his mission on earth needed
to be fulfilled.

Consider your circle. How often do you step out of your comfort zone and mingle with people who look and act differently than you do and who do not agree with you?

Uniformity is not helpful for instinctive, heart-felt living. I have learned the importance of combining all of life's ingredients with the inner wisdom that God has given me if I expect to thrive. One of those lessons was to diversify exposure. There is value in diversity.

Financial planners always say that you should diversify your portfolio. In other words, don't put all of your eggs in one basket. If you do, and something happens to that basket, all of your eggs will be gone. But if you have many baskets with a few eggs in each of them, you won't lose everything if something happens to one of the baskets.

Diversifying your relationships brings you different perspectives and experiences; it causes you to think outside your box and act spontaneously, authentically. It is often harder to work with people who are different from you, but use Jesus' example as a guide. Even though he knew their faults—as well as their strengths—Jesus purposely chose a motley crew of disciples. There was value in diversity!

Prayer
Holy God, thank you for diversity. Thank you for creating us with different ideas, experiences, and perspectives. Help me to honor your creation by reaching across lines and diversifying.

In Jesus' name. Amen.

AWESOME CREATION

*What is mankind that you are mindful of them, human
beings that you care for them? You have made them a little
lower than the angels and crowned them with glory and
honor. You made them rulers over the works of your hands;
you put everything under their feet: all flocks and herds, and
the animals of the wild, the birds in the sky, and the fish in
the sea, all that swim the paths of the seas.*
Psalm 8:4-8, NIV

Scientists say instinct is interwoven into the very fiber of
our DNA! Even our cells have instincts.

Consider our makeup. Our cells' function is based on
what has been genetically programmed within them. Our
cells know how and when to join together and perform
their designated functions. They don't need a conductor
to tell them when to join forces; they just form. They draw
together and beat together to the same rhythm.

Your body develops from cells that find their rightful
place because they know what they were made to do!

These cells vibrate to the tempo of their purpose even before they're operating and performing their function.

What about your inner wisdom about your strengths, abilities, talents, and unique contribution to the world? Are you in sync with them, or is your life somehow offbeat to your inner melody? Have you lost your rhythm because you have not found your place to define and activate your unique contribution?

Seek wisdom from your almighty and awesome Creator in order to follow your instinct. God created your awesome body and crowned you with honor and glory. As David says in Psalm 8, you are a marvelous piece of work—you are specially created in an awesome fashion. Consider God's works—the heavens, the stars, the moon; yet the human body is considered the most special creation. God designed your cells to do what they do—instinctively.

Take a clue from your body and follow your instincts. It's a mighty good way to thank God for creating you. Function in your gift. Perform to the best of your ability each and every day. And keep learning, keep seeking ways to improve, keep listening to your instinct; it holds the key to living a fulfilled life that honors God and does some great work. It's what you were designed for.

Prayer
My God, my God, how wonderful are your works! Thank

you for creating me as a part of your marvelous creation. Thank you for each of my cells and how they instinctively function. I joyously commit to follow my instincts and bring you glory and honor.

In Jesus' name. Amen.

47

FAITH-FILLED FOLLOWER

*"You are the salt of the earth. But if the salt loses its saltiness,
how can it be made salty again? It is no longer good for anything,
except to be thrown out and trampled underfoot. "You are the
light of the world. A town built on a hill cannot be hidden. Neither do people light a lamp and put it under a bowl. Instead they
put it on its stand, and it gives light to everyone in the house."*
Matthew 5:13-15, NIV

Can you imagine a world of instinct followers who
are filled with faith in God? Instincts can lead to a
much more fulfilling life, one that benefits everyone in your life.

Not having the faith to step out and follow instincts is
akin to salt without saltiness. Jesus says in Matthew that if
salt loses its saltiness, it is not good for anything. If salt is
meant to season and preserve, it is pointless if it can't season or preserve. And without that ability, it is not fulfilling
what it was designed to do. Whether you are a manager or
an employee, homemaker or home builder, what matters

most is that you have been awakened to your calling and the inner fulfillment of doing what you were destined to do.

Early in my life, I was haunted by feelings that I was created for more than I could achieve in my environment. The only reason I moved beyond the many potholes and pit stops I encountered is because of an instinctive allure pulling me toward something up ahead on the road that I had to find! I refused to stop and settle for less than an explosive exploration of what God had placed within me.

There is no secret formula for learning to listen to your instincts to pursue the deeper and fuller life you were created to attain. I merely offer you my sparks toward kindling your own blaze.

Are you following your instincts? Are you doing what you were created to do? Don't be unsalty salt. Instead, tap into your God-given instincts and discover true fulfillment. This way you will be a light to others. You will be able to shine and give others a reason to be encouraged and follow their instincts.

Prayer
Dear God, thank you for creating me with a passion.
Teach me to follow my passion and you so that I can
bring honor to your kingdom.
Amen.

48

WORK ETHIC

Whatever you do, work at it with all your heart, as working for the Lord, not for human masters, since you know that you will receive an inheritance from the Lord as a reward. It is the Lord Christ you are serving.
Colossians 3:23-24, NIV

Following your instinct can mean the difference between a job and a career, a place of employment and a rendezvous with destiny. It takes time and lots of effort to do the soul searching required for finding the clues to unlock our fullest and best potential. It is easier to simply fill out a job application, get a good salary, and go to work for someone who has found the thing they were created to do.

This inward urging or prompting of instinct is far too often underutilized; consequently, so many people feel stuck at a certain stage even as they long to be more productive. Living by instinct requires that you search your soul continuously for clues to direct you toward your calling and to pursue your passions. It calls for you to maximize your findings—time and time again. It's not about simply collecting the data about yourself; it is putting instinct into action to become the best you and to create the best opportunities for your passion to flourish.

Not everyone who lives according to instinct is called to be out front—the lead singer, the president, the MVP on the team. Many instinct followers are a part of the support staff for more prominent people. But in their supportive roles, they followed their inner drive and paid attention to their wiring to know how to do their very best. They are more fulfilled and therefore happier so they do better work. Oftentimes, they do the more vital work because what they are doing helps the front person—the one we see—operate his or her gifts.

Whatever your role may be, support or lead, know that you are called to work for God. Your reward will come from the Lord. So use your gifts to bring glory and honor to your Creator.

Paul urges Christians to work with all of their heart. He doesn't mention the job or the importance of it. In Colossians, he was encouraging everyone to work hard and to consider their work as representing Christ. When Christians do good work, excellent work, and outstanding work, it speaks volumes and can show the Christ in them.

It's like representing a college. People tend to hire folks from colleges where they know successful people have attended. It's not that the college prepares all of its students the same or that every graduate from that school is excellent, but they are riding on the reputation of the school—the reputation their predecessors set. So, in whatever it is you're doing, fight the urge to give in to the mundane and routine. Instead work hard. Look for your passions and follow your instincts—even to make a routine job less routine and more stellar.

Whether you work in a government office, a cubicle, a courthouse, or the corner of your apartment, your instincts know truths that can enhance your performance and increase your productivity. There is one thing that is needed to find fulfillment in life—to find that place in life, that station of being, where all that is within you resonates with the challenge before you. This is the spot where inborn natural creativity soars into the horizon of possibility! It's the extra edge that instinct followers use!

Prayer
Dear Lord, I know that I represent you in all I do; therefore, I desire to work unto you—with excellence. Thank you for the opportunity to find my passions and live by instinct.
In Jesus' name. Amen.

49

BUILD BRIDGES

Now faith is the substance of things hoped for, the evidence of things not seen. For by it the elders obtained a good report.

Hebrews 11:1-2, KJV

Instincts can be seen as a bridge—the structure we can use to cross from where we are to where we'd like to be. Instinct can enable you to "see" a healthy relationship, a fulfilling career, and a great opportunity—even if it is not present at the time. Instinct acts much like faith; it sees what is not there, but still hopes for it and expects it.

As a poor child growing up in West Virginia, I was inspired through the absence of the obvious to tap into the presence of the imagined. I remain grateful to this day that I was given that backyard wilderness to teach me to dream of what could be without getting lost in what is. Little did I know that, standing in creek water surrounded by scampering rabbits and hawks gingerly perched on branches, I would playfully start a cycle of innovation that would one day be the mother of my own creative instinct!

Later, as a young pastor, I used this same sheer instinct to step into a condemned building and look beyond the deplorable stench and dilapidated walls of its present condition and see what it could be if given some remodeling, care, and enhancement. My instinct served as a bridge to see more. My instinct became the impetus for a vision, for the power of imagining its potential, and for the tactical steps needed to create a plan of fulfillment.

As I got older, the same instinct that remodeled the building later became the impetus through which I could salvage a flailing company or enhance a weak script into a blockbuster movie.

Scripture speaks of this bridge as faith. It's the seeing when we don't see. What we envision, what we believe will exist. Think about your faith eyesight. Some people can only believe what they can see and touch and feel and smell. But with faith, you can look at what is not visible and see more. If you don't have faith, ask God to heal your unbelief.

Instinct and imagination become the parents of our creative visions. Together, they allow us to see opportunities where others see only limitations. Instead of focusing on what we don't have, we concentrate on what we do have— and what can be created from those ingredients. People with great instincts always transform what they are given into more than what it was when presented to them!

The best thinkers, builders, draftsmen, architects, designers, hairstylists, preachers, and chefs are those who walk amongst us with one foot in reality and the other planted firmly in the realm of the potential. If, like them, you're blessed to recognize the gap between where you are and where you want to be, then you may also know that in order to cross over into a more successful, fully-realized life you must allow your instincts to become your bridge.

Our instincts teach us how to take less and do more. Like a gourmet chef with a limited pantry, we combine the various flavors to create something new and delicious. Our instincts up the ante and propel us to the next level. Our instincts illuminate our path amid the bleakness of realities, statistics, and studies and guide us from the mundane to the magical. Go on and cross that bridge!

Prayer
God in heaven, thank you for the examples of faith followers in the Bible and in my life. I want to see the possible within the impossible.
Amen.

50

SLOW RELEASE

It is a trap to dedicate something rashly and only later to consider one's vows.
Proverbs 20:25, NIV

Enthusiasm without knowledge is no good; haste makes mistakes.
Proverbs 19:2, NLT

The plans of the diligent lead to profit.
Proverbs 21:5a, NIV

Sometimes people jump from the nest and fly. But it's equally important to understand that it is also okay to stroll out of our cage, explore the terrain, return to our cage for a while, explore the freedom again, and so on, until we can navigate the wilderness and forge a way forward. This is a much more balanced and practical approach to leaving your safety zone; it's about your timing and pacing.

You don't have to rush to do everything. Scripture calls rash thinking a "trap." Wisdom and discernment are needed to know how quickly—or slowly—to act. In other words, you can be wholehearted in pursuing where your instincts are leading you and still be practical.

Instinct helps us look ahead and anticipate what we can handle. Some people think they need to quit their job and start a business—without any cash on hand or solid plans for getting any. This is not wise. Instead of jumping feet first without planning, perhaps it is wiser to begin the business on the side or partner with someone who is in a different phase or look for a job that will get you one step closer to your goal. It's taking baby steps toward that goal rather than being rash and jumping all in at once. You can start following your passions without throwing away your stability. Diligence will be rewarded, according to Scripture. It's not how fast you run but how diligent you are that matters most.

When you take baby steps, you discover the strength of your legs before you try to run. You're still on a high wire, but there's a safety net if you fall. This is a safer model of leaving your cage; it balances the external realities of your responsibilities with the relentless longing of your internal instincts. Knowing your pace is also instinctive.

Please understand that following your instincts does not mean you have to make a dramatic departure from everything that you currently consider your cage. My friends in publishing tell me how many people they encounter who quit their day jobs so that they can write best sellers—even though they know nothing about publishing and very little about writing! Similarly, my friends in the music world describe individuals who leave everything behind and yet have not prepared themselves for the realities as they compete for performance opportunities and producers' attention.

So look before you leap. Sometimes it's better to remain in the cage until after feeding time rather than risk starving in the wild! Consider your vows and commitments now— not later. It can help you avoid rash decisions.

Prayer
My Lord, thank you for reminding me to consider pacing when taking a leap out of my comfort zone. Give me wisdom and discernment to know when and how and how fast to leap.
In Jesus' name. Amen.

51

YOU HAVE WHAT IT TAKES

Not only so, but we also glory in our sufferings, because we know that suffering produces perseverance; perseverance, character; and character, hope. And hope does not put us to shame, because God's love has been poured out into our hearts through the Holy Spirit, who has been given to us.
Romans 5:3-5, NIV

Transitions can help us prepare to live instinctively; they can even push us to follow a dream, a passion, or an inclination. Transition can lead to fulfillment in ways we never thought possible.

Although we often resist transitions as negative, we do so because we have the confusion of being unsettled and forced to discover new sets of skills. If we are willing to trust our instincts and act on them, we can adjust. God has created us with varied tools for survival, both intellectually and instinctively.

So instead of seeing a layoff as a loss, consider it to be an opportunity to live instinctively and discover new possibilities. No matter how gifted you were at receiving income one way, you can still unearth the creativity and passion to receive it another way. If a relationship ends or faces a huge challenge, think differently about the challenge. What can you learn from this rough patch? What will you do differently next time? What could this challenge be uncovering in you, in the way you are wired? What if you discovered something previously undiscovered, something God placed inside of you to fuel your destiny?

It's how Paul counseled the Romans to consider suffering. Instead of whining and complaining and seeing suffering as painful, Paul said it's better to focus on the result of suffering. Suffering makes us endure (persevere). And enduring can be good. Why? Because it develops character. Ask anyone whom you consider to be strong to tell you how they got that way, and I'm sure they will show you their battle scars. Strength only comes from heavy lifting. In turn, character is developed under the fire, like a diamond.

In the midst of trials and suffering, it is hard to see how you are growing stronger; but look back over your life and see where and when and how you grew the most. Your growth was probably directly related to a trial or a difficult season. When we view our trials as opportunities for growth, we gain perspective and can carry the load with a renewed mind and with renewed strength.

Finally, Paul says that suffering can lead to hope—hope

for better, hope in God's divine plans to bring out the good in us. For truly all things work together for good (Romans 8:28).

You have what it takes—buried inside of you—to persevere, develop sterling character, and be full of hope for the future. At your core, you are ultimately a survivor. As transition constantly thrusts you into new challenges, you perpetually rediscover dormant capabilities that you didn't realize lay within you. Your challenges can teach you something and bring out qualities you never knew you had.

Consider these challenges as lessons in the classroom. Show up for class and see what you have inside of you to pass the test.

❂ ❂ ❂ ❂

Prayer
I commit myself to not complain or whine when I face
trouble but to face transitions with hope. Thank you
for producing in me perseverance, character, and hope
through suffering.
In Jesus' name. Amen.

52

JUMPERS

Don't let anyone think less of you because you are young.
Be an example to all believers in what you say, in the way
you live, in your love, your faith, and your purity. Until I get
there, focus on reading the Scriptures to the church, encour-
aging the believers, and teaching them.
1 Timothy 4:12-13, NLT

As I study those who follow instincts, I've encountered a type of person I call "jumpers" because
they are willing to jump out of their nests or run
out of their cages. These folks don't necessarily need a
push like the eaglet. They are naturally ready to take risks.

A quotation from a famous jumper sums up his instinctive philosophy on life: "Your time is limited, so don't waste
it living someone else's life. Don't be trapped by dogma—
which is living with the results of other people's thinking.
Don't let the noise of others' opinions drown out your own
inner voice. And most importantly, have the courage to
follow your heart and your intuition. They somehow al-

ready know what you truly want to become. Everything else is secondary." This statement comes from one of the most visionary people of our time, Apple founder Steve Jobs. By jumping, Jobs created one of the most recognizable brands in the world—without even completing college.

Jumpers have learned to move to their own beat and risk when others might not. Jumpers have the courage to follow their heart and pursue their gifts, like Paul instructed Timothy. He told him not to worry about his age and not to let others look down on him because of his age. The same message holds for you. Whether old or young, jumpers only listen to others to the extent that those opinions do not drown out their own inner intuition.

Paul gave Timothy some practical advice when telling him to remain true to his calling, and we can use that advice to jump into the opportunities we need. Paul suggested Timothy devote himself to studying Scripture—getting to know God and God's Word better, which can also lead to confirming our gifts and passions. If we hear more of God's words, we can hear less of naysayers. To follow instincts, we need to be in tune with the Creator, who imbedded instincts in us in the beginning, when God knit us together in the womb (Psalm 139:13).

❂ ❂ ❂ ❂

Prayer

Awesome God, I continue to thank and praise you for creating me with instincts. Help me to follow you and you alone. Help me to drown out distractors and focus on what you've placed inside of me.

In Jesus' name. Amen.

53

CUT AND PRUNE

"I am the true vine, and my Father is the gardener. He cuts off every branch in me that bears no fruit, while every branch that does bear fruit he prunes so that it will be even more fruitful."

John 15:1-2, NIV

On my safari I saw many surprising scenes but none more stunning than listening to our zoologist describe the elephants' waste. Yes, the animal dung had some powerful lessons within it. Our zoologist stopped and told me how much we can learn from the droppings animals left behind. He said their waste provides a high-tech system of clues revealing the who, what, when, and where of the animals in the region. I never knew something that smells so bad could be so smart!

But the thought of tracking the future by looking at the remains of the past captivated me. If we want an instinctive understanding about where we're going, then we must become aware of what we've left behind. Clues aren't always found in the pretty things we've done. Sometimes the greatest insight emerges from the mistakes made and opportunities wasted.

Think about the times you had it really hard. These could have been times when you made mistakes—and perhaps some habits needed to be cut off by the Master Gardener. There may have been habits that you needed to rid yourself of and a circumstance pushed you to do it. You weren't bearing fruit in this area and some things needed to go. You can learn from the past.

In addition to pruning the fruitless areas of our lives, our Gardener also prunes us in places where we need more work or where perhaps we need to ripen and mature. Through trials and tribulations, we can gain newfound strengths and help.

Review your past and see what lessons you've learned. Most psychologists assert that the best predictor of future behavior is past behavior. This doesn't mean you will do the same thing again. However, if we want to change and avoid repeating past failures, we must learn to read our past the same way my guide read what the elephants left behind.

I doubt the animals had any idea that they left so many clues about their identity and future behavior. And as crazy as it may sound, I'm convinced that we leave behind the same kinds of clues. Examine the evidence behind you. Finding out what works and doesn't work in life has a lot to do with understanding yourself. It isn't enough to examine the hearts and minds of others; you must examine your own, as well.

❁ ❁ ❁ ❁

Prayer
I know that God cares for me and desires that I produce fruit. I understand that the pruning process is vital to my growth. Even when it is hard, I know you are cutting some things out of my life and using the tough stuff to strengthen me. I will produce the fruit you desire to live instinctively and to give you glory.
Amen.

54

PRESS FORWARD

Brothers and sisters, I do not consider myself yet to have taken hold of it. But one thing I do: Forgetting what is behind and straining toward what is ahead, I press on toward the goal to win the prize for which God has called me heavenward in Christ Jesus.
Philippians 3:13-14, NIV

The Apostle Paul gave specific instructions about leaving the comforts of the past and pressing on to what beckons us. He was leaving behind a past of unbelief and pressing forward with faith to obtain what God has promised through Christ. And we can use Paul's attitude and words to press past the conformity of the cage into freedom. We can use our faith to explore unknown places—even at the risk of leaving comfort.

And there is comfort in leaving the past behind. It's growth and it is instinctive. Consider the turtles who hatch on a beach and automatically move toward the ocean. They instinctively know that they can't stay where they were born. And likewise, true followers of instinct know that nothing on earth is permanent and look to the new world of change and movement with hope and anticipation.

While past accomplishments and successes are nice to acknowledge, we can't get so caught up in the past that it paralyzes us and forces us to remain in the same stage and state. This life is a journey, one where we are ever seeking to attain all God has laid out for us.

Going out into the wild frontier of possibilities means you have to wean yourself from the nurturing state of normal and accepted practices. All of life is available to us, but not everyone will go through what it takes to enlarge our lives and reshape our environment so that we can release our instincts.

Visit your local zoo, and there you will see animals living in cages. As long as the animal—say, a lion—stays in the cage, he knows exactly when he will eat. Zookeepers provide security. Cages are comfortable. Caged life is consistent. And generally zoos are safe. And yet I suspect there's an urge within our golden-maned friend to see what's beyond the safety of his warm bed and conveniently placed water trough in the cage's corner.

For the animal born in captivity, there's no basis for comparison. His needs are met and he is safe. But if the cage were truly natural, then why must it remain locked? Keepers lock cages because animals are instinctively drawn to freedom, even if they have never lived in the wilderness.

The lion longs for something he may never have experienced, even when his needs are met in the cage.

This is the roar of the entrepreneur. It's not that she can't get a job and be safe. It is that he is attracted to the frontier beyond the cage. The comfort of present limitations may be safe; but where there's nothing ventured, there's, of course, nothing gained. Most creative innovators eventually migrate from the familiar cage of controlled environments into the wild and, yes, dangerous frontier of entrepreneurship.

Whatever tickles your instincts will be something powerful and persistent. Regardless of where your instincts may lead, the question remains the same: do you have the courage to adapt to the wild after living in the cage? Or to put it another way, what do you do when your experiences conflict with your instincts? What if you're raised in an urban area but have instincts for the suburbs? It's the lion's dilemma. If you were trained for a job but have the longing to be an entrepreneur, you feel his pain. If you long to be in a loving, stable relationship but have only known break-ups and heartbreak, then you see through the lion's eyes.

Gird yourself, dig deeply, and prepare to move forward—and never stop moving. What you desire, what you are called to do, and be is on the other side; so press through!

✪ ✪ ✪ ✪

Prayer

All-knowing and loving God, I desire to move forward, to forget my past and press on. I do not want past mistakes or past accomplishments to prevent me from taking hold of all you have called me to do. This day, I declare that I will move forward with your help and never turn back.

In Jesus' name. Amen.

55

USE FEAR

This is why I remind you to fan into flames the spiritual gift God gave you when I laid my hands on you. For God has not given us a spirit of fear and timidity, but of power, love, and self-discipline.

2 Timothy 1:6-7, NLT

Following your instincts take guts. It's not for the timid or the weak. It's for those who are faith-filled and courageous and risk takers. We shouldn't allow our fears to stop us from pursuing what God has placed in us, like Paul instructed Timothy, but there is a time we can use fear. When your fear of living a mundane, average, ineffective life outweighs the fear of staying in your cage, you will have to act. You will have to stir up the gifts God has placed inside of you and make a change—leave the cage of comfort.

And while you are making these changes—because you are too afraid to stay the same—beware of those around you who will not want you to change. A caged lion never mates with a free one. There's something different about people living in cages and people roaming free, exploring new territories, and instinctively following God's plans for their lives. Be aware that you will not be able to run with the same pack—and this applies to business associates, community members, friends, family, and your mind set. You will need new tools to think like a free person who is not restricted to the cage of comfort and the cage of normalcy. To follow your instincts, you will often have to stop your own negativity and doubt—the stuff that is circulating right in your own mind.

Again, you can turn to Paul's wise words and remember to stir up your gifts—your God-given talents—and squash fear and the lack of confidence. Look to God for power, love, and discipline—the stuff it will take to get things done. Look to God to empower you when you feel especially weak and scared. For truly, when we are weak, our Lord's strength is made perfect (2 Corinthians 12:9).

I use fear to keep me moving forward, to make me call upon God for strength. I am not as afraid of dying as many people. I learned early that death is a part of life. My greatest fear is not living before I die, of playing everything so safe that even though I had no risk I also enjoyed no reward.

Face your fears and ask what you will regret the most. The Olympic race of fear within you has but two contenders. One is the claustrophobic fear of staying in the mundane, and the other is the heart-pounding, adrenaline-releasing fear of stepping into the unknown. This race is especially close when instincts take you where your history forsakes you. And there you are left alone with the frightening prospects of what feels foreign and yet entices.

I am afraid of spending my whole life with the deceptive deduction that my cage is the world! So when death tolls and life's ending buzzer shrilly ends my tournament, more tragic than the end of the temporal would be the eternal hypotheticals of "what if?" When I consider such a fate, the hell of regret singes my soul. The agonizing anguish of wondering what I might've been or done if I'd had the courage to free myself from learned behaviors and the cages of my life is wind beneath my wings! I'm not talking about just the cages of calling and careers but something much more significant: the cage of contained thought. The sanctity of the orthodox, succumbing to living in the land of the average, seems a massive waste.

Make the decision today to stir up your gifts and leave the slow, deathly lull of conformity and comfort. Don't let fear stand in your way. Not only have you been given gifts, you have been given power, love, and self-discipline. That's plenty!

Prayer
All-powerful One, I have decided on this day to follow you and to use the gifts you have so graciously given me.

Stir up my gifts. Give me all the power, love, and self-discipline I will need to keep following my instincts and using what you have given me. I am so happy that you are my strength and my power and my glory. I will live this life without regrets.

Amen.

56

DON'T TURN BACK

*That night all the members of the community raised their voices and wept aloud. All the Israelites grumbled against Moses and Aaron, and the whole assembly said to them, "If only we had died in Egypt! Or in this wilderness! Why is the L*ORD *bringing us to this land only to let us fall by the sword? Our wives and children will be taken as plunder. Wouldn't it be better for us to go back to Egypt?" And they said to each other, "We should choose a leader and go back to Egypt."*

Numbers 14:1-4, NIV

Forget the former things; do not dwell on the past. See, I am doing a new thing! Now it springs up; do you not perceive it? I am making a way in the wilderness and streams in the wasteland.

Isaiah 43:18-19, NIV

As terrifying as it may be, sometimes the best thing in the world that can happen to us is for the cage door of comfort and complacency to slam shut. When the door closes on yesterday, we must bring our energies to today. When we can't go back, we're forced to go forward! Without the safety of the cage tempting us to reverse course, we must bring all that we are—our creativity, resiliency, innovation, and resourcefulness—to our new, uncaged life. Sometimes we will never learn to follow our instinct and step into new territories if we are not pushed.

One of the best things that ever happened to the Children of Israel was when God closed the Red Sea after their triumphant exodus out of Egypt. The water opened before them so that they could escape, but it also closed behind them, preventing them from returning. During the forty years it took them to reach the Promised Land, many of them grumbled and complained that their lives were better back in Egypt—despite the fact that they had been slaves there! But reaching this point of no return required them to depend on God's provision and one another in ways that returning to Egypt—or going immediately to the Promised Land—never would have.

Oftentimes, what seems like a hard road will teach us a lesson we needed to learn—or couldn't have learned any other way.

God's Word is filled with examples of God's people needing to move forward, whether they did it kicking and screaming or not. They couldn't turn back—even when they wanted to. We can gain confidence from their stories that just as God was with them then, God is with us now. In Isaiah, God tells the people in exile to focus on the new thing, not the past. The Lord doesn't want the people to remember the old times, the old hardships, but instead God wants them to focus on all he is providing and doing in their lives.

When you find yourself at a crossroad, take comfort in God's Word and God's provision. Our God will do a new thing; your role is to trust and step out and activate your instinct.

When there's no turning back, your instincts will lead you forward. When there's no turning back, you will find a way to stir up what's inside of you and push. So don't act like the Israelites and grumble and wonder if you should return to your cage—that's where slavery and the wilderness are. Instead dig deep and press forward, knowing that good lessons are to be learned from these circumstances.

Reflect on the things you are facing or will face as you leave your cage of comfort. Decide today to adapt an attitude to press forward and not turn back.

❂ ❂ ❂ ❂

Prayer
My God, forgive me for grumbling and complaining.
While I may not be able to see what I'm learning from
my current challenge, help me to dig deep and press
forward. Thank you for giving me all I need.
In Jesus' name. Amen.

57

GOD IS A KEEPER

If you do what the LORD wants, he will make certain each step you take is sure. The LORD will hold your hand, and if you stumble, you still won't fall.
Psalm 37:23-24, CEV

It's perfectly normal to be terrified of making changes. And it's certainly customary to stumble, fall, and have to get up again and again as you make your way through your new environment. You will have to do this time and time again as you learn to live by instinct. But don't get caught up in the falling; don't let a trip keep you down. Get up and keep it moving—each time you fall.

As you leave your cage, the transition will definitely be challenging. You take a few steps forward and few back. You stumble and fall and get back on your feet. Such is the way we learn to lean forward and keep stumbling toward success. It is okay to struggle as you leave the cage and acclimate to the new wilderness before you. Toddlers typically stumble, bumble, and trip before learning to walk. But they keep getting back on their feet and tottering forward until they no longer have to think about keeping their balance. Similarly, when learning to ride a bicycle, whether it be as a child or an adult, one is bound to lose control and crash until the complexity of simultaneous skills becomes second nature.

Many people do not get admitted to college, pass the bar, or become licensed in their field until after several failed attempts. But they persevere, undeterred, wiser and more committed to achieving their goal than they were in the previous attempt.

And again, your faith is critical here—as with everything. Scripture says Christ is able to keep us from falling—or to keep us on our feet. When you are weary and tired and wondering which way to turn, turn to God. Ask him to remind you of the meaning of your life, pick you up, and help you to stand. He's able to keep you standing when you want to fall.

If you are following your God-given purpose, you'll have to succeed. What God wants you to do, God will equip you to accomplish. Where we might trip is when we have visions and plans that don't work out as we imagine. But God's ways are so not our ways. Scripture says 1,000 years to us is like one day with God (and vice versa; see 2 Peter 3:8). Don't use your clock when determining how and when things should happen. Rely on God's timing. So if you fall, get back up. If you feel yourself falling, ask God to keep you standing. He is able to keep you.

❀ ❀ ❀ ❀

Prayer
Almighty God, I am grateful that you are a keeper. Following my instinct and leaving the cage is not easy, but I know that you can keep me. When I stumble or fall, I know you will pick me up and set me on my way. As I faithfully step out into new territories, I keep my hands in your hand and my eyes fixed upon you for strength, comfort, and power.
Amen.

58

SHAKE UP YOUR INSTINCTS

*Search me, God, and know my heart; test me and know my
anxious thoughts. See if there is any offensive way in me,
and lead me in the way everlasting.*
Psalm 139:23-24, NIV

Oftentimes, we find ourselves complacent and paralyzed by the tasks we face each day. We are not
passionate about them, but neither do we know
how to find our passions. So how do we ignite our instincts?

In *Instinct*, I share a favorite story by Joseph Garlington,
a highly revered theologian and speaker from Pittsburgh.
He shared this story with us about his grandchildren. As a
grandfather myself, I can now relate to his story. Perhaps
you've had those moments as well, when the children or
grandchildren are bored playing alone and you are trying
to focus on another task. Subconsciously you notice they
are skipping around, trying to get your attention as you try

even harder to concentrate on your assignment.

The kids could be running up and down the stairs or dashing in and out of a nearby room—waiting to catch your eye. Finally, you look up from what you are doing and catch them by surprise and scream: "Boo!"

They are thrilled! You, assuming you've engaged them enough in that moment, return to your work at hand. But soon, you notice them doing the same things as before— tapping their feet, trying to catch your eye and your attention. They wait on the steps for you to look up again. And if you do not, the grandchild, weary of waiting, will exclaim: "Scare me again, Grandpa! Scare me again!"

The children in this lovely story are just like us. Many gifted and talented people are waiting with instincts that are hungry for a challenge, for stimulation. Our instincts are crying out: Make me study again. Challenge me with something special that will make me grow. Give me something to make me think and work, create and develop. Help me jump out of bed with anticipation again.

Many of us need to cry out to God and ask for our gifts to be stirred, shaken up, and brought back to life. We say, just as the psalmist said, Search me, Lord, and know my heart—those things that incline me to be challenged; try me and know my thoughts—anxious ones, thirsty ones, the ones that will challenge me.

Try calling out to God to help find your challenge—so you can be awakened to your passion. There's a better life to live!

Prayer
Dear Lord, search my heart and make known the passions that lie within. Try my thoughts and show me what challenges me and inspires me. I desire to live a more full and complete life.
In Jesus' name. Amen.

59

URGES AND INSTINCT

Jesus continued: "There was a man who had two sons. The younger one said to his father, 'Father, give me my share of the estate.' So he divided his property between them.

"Not long after that, the younger son got together all he had, set off for a distant country and there squandered his wealth in wild living. After he had spent everything, there was a severe famine in that whole country, and he began to be in need. So he went and hired himself out to a citizen of that country, who sent him to his fields to feed pigs. He longed to fill his stomach with the pods that the pigs were eating, but no one gave him anything.

"When he came to his senses, he said, 'How many of my father's hired servants have food to spare, and here I am starving to death! I will set out and go back to my father and say to him: Father, I have sinned against heaven and against you. I am no longer worthy to be called your son; make me like one of your hired servants.' So he got up and went to his father. "But while he was still a long way off, his father saw him and was filled with compassion for him; he ran to his son, threw his arms around him and kissed him."

Luke 15:11-20, NIV

You may be familiar with this parable that Jesus told about the prodigal son. The young man in this story is a great example of what happens when we live by urges rather than instinct. He can teach us several lessons as we journey toward instinctive living.

First of all, the young man followed his urges, not instinct, when he asked his father for his share of the estate. He wanted to spend his inheritance now and enjoy himself. He set out to live a wild life. But urges are clearly only temporary—and eventually his money ran out. Urges make withdrawals, not deposits, and we know what happens when we only withdraw from an account. The young man ran out of money and found himself needing to work, and the only work he found was feeding the pigs. He was hanging around pigs! He was hanging out with what Jews considered to be an unclean animal.

But he assessed his situation. And you've got to do some assessing in life. Look at who you're comfortable hanging around. Are they people who desire to follow God's will for their lives, to live instinctively, or those who are content living routine, unfulfilled lives? Are your friends more likely to follow urges or instincts? Assess your condition by those around you.

But even when you've been used to living by urges rather than instinct, there is good news. Just as the young man realized who he was and where he came from, you can realize that you are a child of God created with good instincts. You don't have to be a slave to your urges. You can learn to live by your God-given instincts.

Be like the prodigal son and return home—return to your center, your core, your Creator. Ask for forgiveness for living by your urges. Ask for wisdom and discernment to follow your instincts, not urges. Ask God for help and discipline to manage your time and your money. Ask for guidance in uncovering your passions. As you follow instincts, God will give you much more than you can ask for or imagine (Ephesians 3:20).

Follow your instinct. Don't you feel God calling you?

Prayer
God, forgive me for following my urges rather than instinct. Help me to know the difference and to seek you for guidance to live instinctively. I know you are able to exceed my expectations and provide more than I can imagine.
In Jesus' name. Amen.

60

IRON SHARPENERS

As iron sharpens iron, so one person sharpens another.
Proverbs 27:17, NIV

To live by your instincts, you must begin to take inventory of what's on the inside of you as well as who is around you. People who follow instincts are often the most fulfilled people in the room; if you are drawn to them, it could be that you want to be as fulfilled, living out your purpose according to your instinct. These people may not dress a certain way or style their hair alike, but they do appear to be fulfilled—after all following your inner drive leads to true fulfillment. They generally seem happier than those who live below their gifting or those who do not follow their passions. They make decisions that others may think are too risky, they work hard, and they seem invigorated by life. It is well worth it to look for these types of people and to hang out with them. Why?

Scripture says that iron sharpens iron; and people,

places, and perspectives that resonate with us often do so because of a shared, kindred quality. When something or someone you encounter resonates with you, pay attention. Become a student of your deepest passions and persistent curiosities. Notice the people you admire and feel drawn to emulate. We instinctively recognize members of our own tribe, no matter how different they may look! Pay attention to how they make decisions, live their lives, and interact with others. Study them. Ask to be mentored by them. Get sharpened by them.

Just because the goose lays eggs on land doesn't negate the fact that her offspring are drawn to the water. The people who can draw out the good stuff in us may not be just like us—but we could still be drawn to the water or to these people. Look past where you started to discover who you can become and what you can be. Move beyond where you were born to become who you were born to be. Listen to your instincts and you will find your power and your natural inclinations.

Think about the people you are surrounded with. Find the ones who are helpful at drawing out your passions. Stick closely to those who are following their instincts. Find people who have that outward expression of their inward inclinations, and they may sharpen you and help you become an instinct follower, too.

You won't try to follow step-by-step what these iron sharpeners do—after all we are all unique and have unique callings. But you can glean from how they approach life, how they interact with others, and what they study. You can pick up on how they balance instinct and intellect and use what you learn in your own life, in your own way. Iron can always be sharpened. Find those who can bring out the best in you and help you hone your instinct-following skills. The world awaits your contribution.

Prayer
Masterful Creator, teach me to expand my network and expose myself to iron sharpening people. I want to recognize instinct followers and learn from them.
In Jesus' name. Amen.

61

YOU ARE A SURVIVOR

But Joseph said to them, "Don't be afraid. Am I in the place of God? You intended to harm me, but God intended it for good to accomplish what is now being done, the saving of many lives.

Genesis 50:19-20, NIV

Don't let evil get the best of you; get the best of evil by doing good.

Romans 12:21, MSG

When you follow your instincts and transform your vision into reality, you will begin to look at accidents, mistakes, conflicts, and issues differently. Many times, we get upset when things do not go our way or people get in between us and our achievement of what we desire. We can get angry, lash out, or even give up on what we desire. But as you grow and as you follow your instincts more and more, you will realize that mistakes can often lead to success. Accidents can become creative material, waiting to be shaped into success. Conflicts can make you grow, gain new perspective, or find a new, better way. Instinct often processes, learns, and accepts change before we do. And when our emotions, intentions, and abilities catch up—when we stop brooding over what could have been or what happened—we can move forward and one step closer to seeing our dreams realized. You learn that you truly are a survivor, even a thriver!

To better understand this concept of turning mistakes into success, meditate on Joseph's story. The heart of his story starts in Genesis 37, when he is a young man (17 years old). Joseph is a dreamer; he has great thoughts and great ideas. He knows he has been created for greatness (Genesis 37:1-12). Unfortunately this young man tells his dreams to others; and perhaps they are not instinct followers or dreamers themselves, and they do not like his dream. Joseph is sold by his own brothers, which could look like a big mistake, a huge dream-stopping move. But Joseph is a survivor. His hard work, morality, and favor from God shows—even when he is working as a servant. Regardless of what job you do, your true character can shine through!

So Joseph rises to the top ranks even as a servant, but conflict gets him again. His boss' wife wants him (that's in Genesis 39). And while Joseph refuses to give into her, he is still punished because of her. Joseph, the dreamer, now finds himself in prison. But even in confinement, his true colors shine through and he befriends men who promise to help him. When one finally remembers his promise, Joseph is called out of prison to help (Genesis 41). His gift of discerning dreams catapults him to become a leader in Egypt

This power-packed story continues with some rich content and messages about surviving mishaps, mistakes, conflicts, and all sorts of circumstances that could make you give up. In the end, Joseph recognizes that he has been through it all for a reason. He has been brought to this place in Egypt to save his family—the very family that turned their backs on him. And like a true survivor who knows that God truly does work things together for our good (Romans 8:28), Joseph doesn't seek revenge. He blesses those who cursed him. He gets the best of evil by doing good.

A true instinct follower can see past the challenges and hard circumstances to see the creative, provisional hand of God making a way. A survivor makes lemonade and serves it to their haters!

Prayer

All-knowing and All-seeing God, I know that my challenges and trials can make me stronger if I hold on to your hand and follow where you lead me. I will not let mishaps make me bitter or angry. I will use these roadblocks to find creative solutions and new paths. I cling to you for encouragement and help, especially during these times.

In Jesus' name. Amen.

62

LIVE FULLY

I have come that they may have life, and have it to the full.
John 10:10b, NIV

Our instincts are the treasure map for our soul's satisfaction. Following our instincts can make the crucial distinction between what we are good at—our vocation or skill set—and what we are good for—the fulfillment of our potential. When you're truly engaged with your life's calling, you rely on something that cannot be taught. It's a calling—to create, to teach, give, build, to do whatever allows your instinct to guide you to the "something more" that you suspect is in you. If you are following your calling, you are living instinctively.

Your instincts can help you align your unique variables with your callings and release the treasure within you. When harnessed, refined, and heeded, your instincts can provide the key to unlocking your most productive, most satisfying, most joyful life.

It will still require hard work and dedication on your part, but the internal satisfaction will fuel your desire to achieve even larger dreams. Based on the fact that we are all inherently creative people, if you are in touch with your instincts, you will naturally increase in your endeavors.

Christ wants us to have fulfilling lives—for us to live life to the full. Yes, our Lord gives us eternal life, but he wants us to have an abundant life here and now on earth.

When you realize that you are truly created to live fully, you will take the time and put in the hard work to find out what you are wired to do. You can put on your special vision glasses and look back over your life, paying attention to what brought you joy. What made you feel fulfilled, curious, challenged, motivated? Likewise, you can trace your steps and figure out what made you upset. What did you think was unfair? What would you put on boots and march down the street to stop? These are some of the ways you can uncover what makes you tick—and begin to understand your gifts and passion areas. Then you can find ways to exercise these God-given talents; you can find ways to hone them, build them, use them for God's glory. You will get the fulfillment.

✪ ✪ ✪ ✪

Prayer
Loving God, you promised to give us life more abundantly. I will seek high and low to find my calling while I'm here on earth so I may live to the full.

In Jesus' name. Amen.

63

YOUR COMPANY

Walk with the wise and become wise.
                    Proverbs 13:20a, NLT

Therefore walk in the way of the good, and keep to the paths of the just.
                    Proverbs 2:20, NRSV

Oftentimes, when people are trying to live fulfilling lives, they think about success and automatically assume they should follow the lead of successful folk. I don't suggest that we take our script from others. The low-grade plagiarism of popularity will never lead you to true contentment. But we can learn from real risk takers committed to living instinctively, who listen for more than information, see beyond example, and grasp inspiration to ignite their purpose.

This is why I encourage people to study others—to pay attention to how they operate. If you are able, volunteer to help someone you admire, someone who lives by their instincts. You want to get as close as possible to observe how they function. By no means does observing another replace the hard work of digging deep and discovering your inclinations. But walking with the wise can make you wise. Observing instinct followers can point you in the right direction and make you more in tune with following your instincts. Like knows like. Iron sharpens iron, and your companions can either sharpen you or dull your senses.

Look at the company you keep. Make sure you have people in your network who can help you follow your instinct, who can help you become a better person. If you need to upgrade your network, don't be afraid to step out of your comfort zone and find some instinct followers to hang out with.

I truly believe that following your instincts will transform your workplace, liberate your career, and enhance your relationships. It's well worth it to find like-minded people and walk with them. Your instincts will thank you. The world will thank you for your contributions. Your heart will thank you because you will be fulfilled.

Prayer
Faithful God, I know iron sharpens iron and I desire to walk with the wise. Show me instinct followers and help me glean from them as I dig deeper and explore my inner drive.
In Jesus' name. Amen.

64

YOU'VE GOT THE POWER

I want you to know about the great and mighty power that God has for us followers. It is the same wonderful power he used when he raised Christ from death and let him sit at his right side in heaven. There Christ rules over all forces, authorities, powers, and rulers. He rules over all beings in this world and will rule in the future world as well.
Ephesians 1:19-21, CEV

What can we say about all this? If God is on our side, can anyone be against us?
Romans 8:31, CEV

Instinct followers keep going—no matter what. Yes, they will meet obstacles and oppositions; it's a guarantee. But as I studied this amazing and natural phenomena called instinct, I looked at all types of people who have done exceptional things, and they did so in the face of criticisms and oppositions.

Their paths were not always smooth; they didn't always

have the money, the time, the support. It probably never seemed like just the right time to step out and cut a new path down the road. But think about it: if we acquiesced to the status quo, we wouldn't have the airplane, we wouldn't have the steam engine, and we wouldn't have so many of the things that we have today.

Instinct followers do the uncommon stuff even when it isn't comfortable or it doesn't seem like the right time. Instinct followers take risks.

I grew up during the 60s, and trust me when I tell you there were many naysayers to Dr. King, but he instinctively went forward anyway. You cannot use public polls to determine personal purpose. You need to listen carefully to your inner calling, your inner drive. Growing closer and closer to God can help you learn more about yourself and listen for God's timing, not human's timing. Tuning into your Life Giver can give you the strength and impetus to press forward when it seems like everything and everyone is against you.

If God is on your side, who can be against you? In other words, why does it matter who is against you? God's power is strong enough. It's resurrection power—the same wonderful power used to raise Christ from the dead. What is more powerful than that?

Don't let naysayers stop you. Don't let yourself stop you—the negative words you can replay in your mind. Don't let circumstances stop you; it will never be a perfect time to launch out and follow your God-given mission.

Activate your faith, rely on God's amazing power, and know that God is on your side. You have all you need.

✪ ✪ ✪ ✪

Prayer
Powerful and mighty God, I will not let negative words
from others or myself stop me from following my in-
stincts. I desire to live the life you have designed me to
live. I rely on your strength to fulfill my mission.
Amen.

65

USE YOUR INSTINCTS

The LORD is my shepherd, I lack nothing. He makes me lie down in green pastures, he leads me beside quiet waters, he refreshes my soul. He guides me along the right paths for his name's sake.

Psalm 23:1-3, NIV

Being in tune with your instinct moves you to action. Instinctive action comes from utilizing what our creative Creator has invested in our deepest parts. It is "in"-vested in all of us—to adapt, to transform, to create, and to sense moments of significance or danger—moments to be wary and moments to be warring, when to cringe and when to capture, how to craft and not to crash.

It is instinctive action that determines how we manage the moment, move into position and adapt, resourcefully create, and strategically forge ahead without fear. The common denominator of instinct wins presidential elections, makes comedians successful, causes architects to build timeless monuments, and elevates engineers to become artists.

Living by instinct elevates your ability to know where you're going and how to get there. It can help you know when to slow down and step back and when to accelerate and step up. And it can guide you to what you're ultimately looking for—a fulfilled life.

Walking with God will sharpen your instincts. You are like David as he penned the popular 23rd Psalm. If you see yourself as a sheep, willing to be guided by your Great Shepherd, God, you will faithfully follow where your Lord leads. God can lead you through your instincts so following the Great Shepherd can activate your instincts.

Walk closely with the Shepherd. Trust him to lead you even when you can't see. Lean on the testimonies of those in the Bible and those in your life who have allowed the' Shepherd to lead them along green pastures—even when it seemed they were passing through the valley of death. Do what your Shepherd says to do and go where he says to go.

Spend some time getting to know your Shepherd better, and your trust and faith will grow—large enough to activate your instinct.

Prayer

Loving Shepherd, thank you for loving me so much that you guide me as my personal shepherd. Thank you for

your promises to walk beside me. I will tap into your amazing power to follow my instincts.

Amen.

66

YOU CAN DO IT

For I can do everything through Christ, who gives me strength.
Philippians 4:13, NLT

By faith we understand that the universe was formed at God's command, so that what is seen was not made out of what was visible. By faith Abel brought God a better offering than Cain did. By faith he was commended as righteous, when God spoke well of his offerings. And by faith Abel still speaks, even though he is dead.
Hebrews 11:3-4, NIV

I pray that out of his glorious riches he may strengthen you with power through his Spirit in your inner being, so that Christ may dwell in your hearts through faith. And I pray that you, being rooted and established in love, may have power, together with all the Lord's holy people, to grasp how wide and long and high and deep is the love of Christ, and to know this love that surpasses knowledge—that you may be filled to the measure of all the fullness of God.
Ephesians 3:16-19, NIV

Use your God-given gifts and follow your instinct!

Pursue your dreams and make them fit within your situation, rather than adapting to your situation if it doesn't feed the stirrings within you. It will take courage and faith to break your tendency to go with the flow and follow the norm, and instead pursue what your instincts reveal is your true destiny. But be encouraged; it is possible—it's more than possible. Many have done it; many are doing it now. With faith, all things are possible (Mark 9:23). And with Christ empowering you, like Paul says, you can do all things. The Lord provides the strength for whatever he has purposed you to do.

Walk through the hall of faith in Hebrews 11. Read about the many people who chose to follow God's direction—oftentimes without understanding or knowing exactly where God was leading them. But, repeatedly, Scripture says they walked "by faith." Their accounts can give you hope and remind you to lean upon God.

Rise up and reclaim your strength. Refocus and gear up to take back your dreams and follow them. God will give you strength to unearth what is already inside of you. You bring the faith, and God will show you the way. You bring the work of delving beyond the norms and adapting to what's around you, and God will give you new insight into what you should be doing, where you should be going, and how you can get there. God is more than capable of giving you all things needed to accomplish what you are called to do. God's love surpasses knowledge and God's strength is immeasurable. You can be fulfilled. You can follow your dreams and live out your calling.

Yes, you have the strength and the courage to do all things.

❁ ❁ ❁ ❁

Prayer
Dear God, I thank you for the reminder that you empower me to do all things. I thank you for the strength to stir up the gifts you have implanted in me at an early age. Give me the courage to follow my instinct.
In Jesus' name. Amen.

67

BE FAITHFUL

"To the faithful you show yourself faithful; to those with integrity you show integrity."
2 Samuel 22:26, NLT

Expose yourself to a wide variety of people. It will help you create your own unique path and follow your particular God-given instincts. Too often, we're not exposed to folk who are truly following their passions. The unexposed have no idea what it looks like to follow dreams, listen to instinct, and act. To activate your instincts, start with exposure. You cannot be what you do not see. It isn't that exposure gives us instincts; it's that exposure awakens instincts and stops us from ignoring what we know to be true within us.

Exposure works much like the old photography film used to (before the great invention of the digital camera). A photographer needed a dark room to take the film out of the camera and expose it so it could become the image that was already on the film. Get it? The photographer had the picture; it was on the film, but it needed to be exposed to the light to fully become the image that was on the film.

That's what many of us need. We need faith to see what's already implanted in us. The picture has already been taken; in fact, it was created within you early on. That's how God created you. But internally, in the dark, the image has not come to light. It has not been exposed.

So how do you get exposure? How do you get exposed to instinct followers who can help you recognize how fulfilling it is to walk in your true calling and follow your inner drive? I've mentioned before that it is vital to pay attention to those you are drawn to, people who seem to have a little extra something. These people go the extra mile—with joy. Their work seems effortless yet impeccable. They seem fulfilled—as if what they are doing is a natural extension of themselves. Find them in your church. Look for them in the community. Listen to them speak at conferences, luncheons, etc. And don't always follow the spotlight. Instinct followers can be seen assisting others, teaching classes, creating pictures, playing with kids, etc. Open your eyes to catch a broad vision of instinct followers.

Pay attention to how they move and work. Grab them and ask a few questions about how they got to the path they are on. Find a mentor. Discuss some of these concepts with him or her. While incorporating some of these steps, eventually your inner proclivities will show through and your vision will be adjusted. You will see what you've searched for. Be faithful; and watch God, in turn, be faithful to help you follow your instinct.

Prayer
Faithful God, I commit to searching for my inborn drive.
I desire to unleash it to live a fulfilling life according to your will and your way. Expose me to people who can help me uncover my life's mission, and I will be faithful to live it out for your glory.
Amen.

68

HANDLE ADVERSITY

They give me understanding and make me hate all lies. Your word is a lamp that gives light wherever I walk. Your laws are fair, and I have given my word to respect them all.
Psalm 119:104-106, CEV

Instinct followers know adversity won't break you. And, if you work it right, your roadblock could lead you to more instinctive ways to get to your goal.

Whether you're running a tech business or a bakery, a hotel chain or your own household, you must filter adversity through your instinct to survive. When results don't run according to plan, you must be willing to change course, adapt your vision, and recalculate what's needed to survive. Every obstacle contains an opportunity. It may not be the doorway to success you were looking for; it may be a second-story window left open just a crack!

Your instincts naturally create a way forward from wherever you are. Hardship can humble you, but it cannot break you unless you let it. Your instinct for survival will see you through if you're attuned to it. Instinct will find a temporary stopgap without ever taking its sights off of your larger goals. There's no greater way to hone your instincts than to overcome adversity.

Reflect on the adversity you face today. Consider the lessons available for you to learn from this trial. Determine that you will use your roadblocks as stepping stones to find a better way, to adapt your vision, and recalculate your route. Commit to drawing closer to God during these times and seeking God's way to overcome hurdles.

Know that your instincts can transform adversity into opportunity. They fully understand what old people said as they quoted Scripture: "Weeping comes at night, but joy comes in the morning" (Psalm 30:5). As you weep and cry and work through adversity, look for the morning light where you can use what you've learned to live a joyful life. It's only going to be night for a short period of time. Look for the morning and follow your instinct.

As a famous quote says: "Don't curse the dark; light a candle." Pick up your light and use it to get through the night. The psalmist calls God's Word a lamp that gives understanding. God's Word gives light wherever we walk. When adversity strikes, look to your light and look to God for understanding. A better way, a bigger lesson is just around the corner. Can you see it?

❂ ❂ ❂ ❂

Prayer
My Light and my Salvation, help me endure the rough
times and see them as a way to build my instincts to follow and trust you to lead me in the right path.
In Jesus' name. Amen.

69

TRAIN WELL

The student is not above the teacher, but everyone who is fully trained will be like their teacher.
Luke 6:40, NIV

We can learn a great deal about following instinct by observing gifted athletes and performers. These people always stretch and extend beyond their present capabilities, using what they've already accomplished as a launching pad. They don't assume they already have what it takes to win—although in most cases it seems as if they do. They know that becoming lazy and complacent can lead to weakness, causing them to perform less than their optimum. So they push. They lift more weights, run more miles, practice more hours. The elite athlete hires a trainer who is experienced in training Olympians or other elite athletes. If they want to get the top award, they follow the training of someone who has already attained it—or, at the very least, helped others to attain it.

Look at your life and how you handle it. Ask yourself if you are ready to be trained for this race. Get ready to lift more weights and do more reps and more sets. Get ready to sweat hard and put in the hours to do what you feel called to do. It takes lots of work; no doubt. But it is all worth it if you want to follow your instinct and live differently and be more fulfilled. Training may feel painful at the moment—and it will definitely take some discipline and will—but you will be better equipped to run this race, to win the race.

Your training starts with getting in contact with your Creator on a new level. Spend some time in prayer. Spend some time engaging in self-awareness—finding out what gets you going, what intrigues you, what you are innately good at. This training is not about becoming self-absorbed, babying your inner child, or excusing self-indulgence. It's simply about whether you have courage to look within yourself and embrace all that you find there.

And again, as I say many times when discussing following God-given instinct: you will need to have faith glasses on. Your vision can not get discouraged by what you see in the now, what you see around you, or what your circumstances say about you.

Your vision needs to see like faith sees. Faith sees the things that are not there…yet. Faith sees the things inside of you that haven't been exercised and developed quite yet.

The world needs your gift, the one that God specially planted within you. Get your training on now. Think of the fulfilled life you can lead.

✪ ✪ ✪ ✪

Prayer
Holy God, I commit myself to spiritual training so that I
may work out what you've put inside of me and be more
in tune with following my instincts.
In Jesus' name. Amen.

SEASONS

And [Daniel] said: "Praise be to the name of God for ever and ever; wisdom and power are his. He changes times and seasons; he deposes kings and raises up others. He gives wisdom to the wise and knowledge to the discerning. He reveals deep and hidden things; he knows what lies in darkness, and light dwells with him.

Daniel 2:20-22, NIV

Change is not always easy, and the need for change is not always plain. Depending on your experience, you may have to embrace change in order to survive; for change is not only expected, but it often signals growth and innovation. Instinct followers often change faster than the people around them.

People who fit at one stage of growth may not seem compatible as you grow, encounter higher ideals, and set new goals.

Instinctively—and painfully—you learn that you can't take everyone with you just because they were with you where you were before. You will likely feel divided, unable to decide whether to obey your heart or your mind! Your instincts will show you when the rules change and how to handle the changes.

If you are still thinking that the people on your team—or in your relationship—are the same as they were yesterday, you need to take an assessment as soon as possible. And just like you have grown and changed, I bet they have too. It could be time to make a shift in the way you do business and the way you relate to those with whom you partner.

It's a wise idea to assess yourself and your team often. It's also wise to remind yourself that change is inevitable and to decide that you are not going to be afraid of it. You're not going to be afraid to have the hard conversations and to make the hard decisions. You are a leader—and that's what you have to do sometimes. Even kings are deposed of sometimes. Instead of fighting against the changing seasons, embrace them. No one would think it made sense to wear the same clothes on a hot summer day as they do in the midst of a winter snowstorm; and likewise, you shouldn't have the exact same team or the exact same approach in different seasons of your life, relationship, or business.

Some folks are with you for a reason, some are with you for a season, and some are with you for a lifetime. Know when to change. Know when to know what season it is—and wear the right clothing.

Prayer
Lord, I am aware of ever-changing relationships. I will
stay connected to you as my anchor, my unchanging
constant, and trust you to help me assess what needs to
change in and around me.
In Jesus' name. Amen.

71

DEPOSITS AND WITHDRAWALS

*"You didn't choose me, remember; I chose you, and put you
in the world to bear fruit, fruit that won't spoil."*
John 15:16a, MSG

Many people grapple with lack. They think they
lack talent, they lack gifts, or they lack the resources to truly live the life God has called them
to live. They don't think they have what it takes to follow
instincts and live out their mission. They settle for less.
They settle for lack luster lives of contentment.

I encourage you to never settle for less than you were
created for—to bear good and healthy and delicious fruit.
God has given us instincts to be attracted to what fits a
higher and better purpose. Never settle for less than God's
best for your life.

I like to think of it this way: God will not ask you to
make a withdrawal if there are insufficient funds. God will
only ask of you what God has already deposited inside of

you. So when you are called to impact others—to discover, develop, and use your gifts and follow your mission—God is only asking you to tap into the account that is within you. God has placed all you need right inside of you. Your job is to develop those gifts, listen carefully to your inclinations, and follow God's leading.

You have what it takes—right inside of you. It's the way God designed you. We all have special gifts. Some are dormant and need to be activated, but God is a generous God who wouldn't create you without depositing something into your core. Our Creator only asks you to use what you already have and to do what you can do with God's amazing power.

Stop saying what you don't have, stop down-playing or ignoring your gifts. It's time you make a withdrawal from all that God has deposited within you. Your withdrawal will be used to share with others, to bless others, and in return will give you a rich and fulfilling life.

Prayer
Provider God, your plans are far greater than anything
I can imagine. I know you've planted seeds inside me to
bear fruit. I will withdraw what you deposited in me so
that I may live according to your will and follow my mission. I will bear good fruit.
Amen.

72

GOD WILL SUPPLY

*And my God will meet all your needs according to the riches
of his glory in Christ Jesus.*
                    Philippians 4:19, NIV

Your instincts are more resourceful, resilient, and responsive than you probably realize; and when ideas hang
out with influence, income will always emerge.

Most people don't pursue their creative, out-of-the-box
ideas for fear of the investment. But a great idea can attract investors. Relationships are our greatest resource.
But those relationships must cross-pollinate beyond the
familiar. You must not limit yourself. You can't be surrounded with monolithic relationships and fully tap into
your potential.

Scripture confirms that God will supply all of our needs.
In faith, we can use instinct to begin the path and start the
journey toward a fulfilling life with the expectation that
God will send the right people with the various resources
we need. God will supply your need.

When you have an instinctive idea, it will die in the crib if you don't assemble a team around it that has similar instincts but diverse perspectives of influence and contribution. The best way to kill your instincts is to surround yourself with only practical people who never take the voyage beyond what the empirical data states. If you only move based on data, you will only regurgitate old ideas. Refer to the data and heed its wisdom when feasible; but sooner or later, all inventors and most investors must ground themselves in their instincts.

And when creative instincts emerge, resources will eventually catch up. Usually, the information has to play catch-up with the inclination. You aren't one bank loan away from a million dollars, but you are one creative idea from a million dollars. When circumstances seem to hold you hostage, your instincts pay the ransom. Use faith to press your way through, and watch exactly what you need show up. God will supply!

Prayer
Awesome Lord, I thank you for always providing exactly
what I need. Forgive me for doubting, and help me step
out on faith and anticipate you meeting my needs.
In Jesus' name. Amen.

73

MEDITATIONS OF THE HEART

The Lord our God be with us, as he was with our fathers:
let him not leave us, nor forsake us: That he may incline
our hearts unto him, to walk in all his ways, and to keep his
commandments, and his statutes, and his judgments, which
he commanded our fathers.
1 Kings 8:57-58, KJV

Doing the work of discovering your God-given gifts and passions is not always intuitive. Even following our instincts needs to be developed. While we're all born with instincts, we are not all born or raised in an environment that helps us to easily recognize our gifts and learn how to incorporate them into our life's mission and work. If we have not had those gifts affirmed by someone else, or even ourselves, we often overlook them.

So how do you find the inner drive, the work that makes you sing? Think about the last time you did something and you felt good about its outcome (a project, etc.). Think about the last time you felt accomplished, even tired, but inspired. Reflect on the last time your eyes lit up or your heart skipped a beat as you performed a task. Think outside of the box to hobbies, community work, conversations, or events. Revisit the place you last felt alive and ask yourself if there are patterns you can trace to see where your passions lie.

Don't run away from the things that made you work hard. Oftentimes, we put in extra effort when it is worth it or when we feel connected and in our zone. Perhaps this was a task that required you to put in more hours than normal, but you enjoyed it—in the end. No one had to make you stay late or get up early to get it completed. Perhaps it could be pointing toward your natural inclination.

Think about the last time you received a compliment about work you had done or a relationship you cultivated. It may not have seemed like a big deal, but your special flair—even unbeknownst to you—made it seem special. People recognized that; and while they may not have affirmed your efforts, their pleasure or even your pleasure can be an affirmation. Check it out and study it.

Keep track of your findings and allow them to guide you down your path. Turn your ears and heart toward God for insight on who you are and what you are created for. God is the Creator and the Keeper of your heart. God knows your passions and desires. Get to know God, and get to know yourself so you can unleash what's inside of you.

✪ ✪ ✪ ✪

Prayer

My Lord and God, get my heart ready to know you better. Prepare my heart to know myself better. I desire to uncover my inner drive so that I may live a fulfilled and inspired life.

In Jesus' name. Amen.

74

LIVE WITHOUT LIMITS

Cast all your anxiety on him because he cares for you.
1 Peter 5:7, NIV

*Rejoice always, pray without ceasing, in everything give
thanks; for this is the will of God in Christ Jesus for you.*
1 Thessalonians 5:16-18, NKJV

Following your instincts is not a one-time thing. You
don't hit it big and stop listening to instincts. True
instinct followers are constantly looking and listening for the right time and the right move. They don't get
complacent and stop following instincts. They put in the
hard work of tuning into their inborn drive and tuning
out negativity and other things that can block them from
passionately pursuing their gifts. This fulfilling way of life
is not a sprint; it is a journey. So it is best to tackle what
is stopping you now and make it a point to wake up each
morning and declare that your fear or anxiety or over reli-

ance on intellect will not keep you from following your instinct.

Find the areas in your journey that cause you anxiety. Explore places you feel insecure and afraid. Turn over your concerns to our faithful God, who cares for all of us and wants us to cast our cares on him. Instinctively listening to God's leading will develop your prayer life. And your prayer life is key in relinquishing your cares to God. Going to the Great Listener consistently reminds you to turn over fear and worry, and instead activate faith.

Scripture reminds us to pray without ceasing. We should pray not only for big decisions, but for every decision. Developing a constant prayer life opens our eyes and hearts to God, which opens us up to special wisdom and discernment. Staying connected to God helps you follow your instinct. And while we're in touch and in tune with God, our prayers and daily living are also filled with joy and gratitude for this journey. We are joyous because we realize our God-given gifts and potential, and we know we cannot truly follow our instincts without being in tune with our Gift Giver.

You can fly and live without limits. Worry, stress, and anxiety do not have to weigh you down. Tap into your powerful stress reliever. Pray and let it go. A new, fulfilling life awaits you.

✪ ✪ ✪ ✪

Prayer

Caring God, right now, I cast my cares upon you. I relinquish any and everything that weighs me down and blocks me from following my instinct. I am grateful that I can pray to you continuously and that you care for me. I am thankful to live this life without limits so that I may fulfill my mission.

Amen.

DON'T LOOK BACK

The person who trusts me will not only do what I'm doing but even greater things, because I, on my way to the Father, am giving you the same work to do that I've been doing. You can count on it. From now on, whatever you request along the lines of who I am and what I am doing, I'll do it.
John 14:12-13, MSG

O ur instincts would rather lead us to face the unknown than back into the comforts of the past. Even when we're unsettled by unfamiliarity and nothing in our repertoire of achievements, abilities, our family, training, education, or experience has prepared us, we are drawn instinctively toward what excites us, touches us, energizes us, and leaves us shaking in our boots. Scripture says we can do "great" things; and somewhere deep in each of us, we know this and desire to reach our God-given potential.

Instinct likes a challenge more than comfort; it's the thing we have been designed for. When we're committed to fulfilling our destiny, our instinct drives us away from complacency and toward deeper contentment.

It doesn't matter whether it's a new career, a new marriage, a new season of being single, or a new business launch. When we start anything by following our instincts, we will likely be forced to leave our cage of comfort and complacency. We must keep moving forward, following our instinct in the bold directions.

As Christians, we have even more resources for living instinctively. God gives us the power. Jesus even says that we will be empowered to do greater things than the miracles and works he did while on earth. When we trust in God and trust in God's plan for our lives, we really can do great things. You can count on it. So start petitioning God to help you fulfill your destiny, to give you all you need to do what you've been called to do. Build your trust, rely on your faith, and do great things. Don't let complacency or fear of moving forward stop you from doing what you are called to do.

It would be terrible to be sidetracked by the comfort of your past because you looked back and let fear paralyze you. Keep following your instinct and don't let the comfort of yesterday make you complacent. Keep moving forward. Keep trusting God.

Prayer
Omnipotent God, keep me looking forward to where you

are leading me at all times. When I am tempted to look back or shrink back into the cage of comfort, increase my faith and trust in you so that I may do great things. I desire to follow the instinct you've carefully placed inside of me.

Amen.

76

THINK HIGHER

"My thoughts are nothing like your thoughts," says the Lord. *"And my ways are far beyond anything you could imagine. For just as the heavens are higher than the earth, so my ways are higher than your ways and my thoughts higher than your thoughts."*
Isaiah 55:8-9, NLT

Oftentimes, our instincts are held captive because our minds just can't conceive why we should do one thing and not the other thing that all the data points to. Information can be very useful and helpful, but also confining if not kept in balance. Instinct followers have to go beyond data and logic to follow God's leading via instinct.

When you feel an alluring attraction, one you finally cannot ignore, it may be God's calling via your instincts if it is consistent with God's Word. Ask God if this is the right direction for you, if it's what God wants for you, and if it's in God's perfect will. Be aware of God's presence and proceed if you hear: "Yes."

Even with the sense of God's calling and blessing, you will likely remain fearful, as I did when I moved to Dallas. As I shared in detail in *Instinct*, I had lived in West Virginia my entire life and would not only be leaving my church to plant a new one, but also leaving one lifestyle and culture for another. I understand your fear, trepidation, and agony over a decision to follow your instincts. It doesn't make sense to give up your comfortable security, and you wonder if you will regret taking the risk when you inevitably confront adversity.

But just as I had to leave my cage, so do you. Take the risk. Not only did I feel God's prompting to make the move, but something deep inside me knew it was where I belonged—even if I didn't exactly know why. Needless to say, I have never regretted my decision to follow my instincts and move to Dallas. No, instead I discovered that my move was not just an open door to me but was in fact the intersection of the destiny of thousands, if not millions, of others whose lives would forever be changed—all predicated upon me releasing my fear and mustering the courage to be stretched beyond my comfort.

Pray and pray and pray. Then ask God for the courage to act and to follow boldly. God always provides—in one way or another. Bring the faith and watch God work.

When you feel God's prompting through your instinct, always remember that God is not human; God does not think like us. God's ways are much higher than ours, and the Almighty's thoughts are higher than ours, too. What God has planned for us doesn't always seem possible or even logical, but that's because we don't think like God! The next time fear and trepidation creep into your God-given plans, look up and try to see just how far the heavens are from the earth and remember how much higher God's thoughts are.

Prayer

God in heaven, I desire to balance logic and instinct.
Incline my heart to listen to you and follow your path
above all else. I know your thoughts are so much higher
than anything I can conceive. Thank you for my journey.
Thank you for always being with me.
In Jesus' name. Amen.

LEARN TO ADAPT

*"The virgin will conceive and give birth to a son, and they
will call him Immanuel" (which means "God with us").*
Matthew 1:23, NIV

And surely I am with you always, to the very end of the age.
Matthew 28:20b, NIV

Instincts under pressure crush the carbon of conformity and create diamonds. Each new season of this training camp we call life offers to train us for the next season if we pay attention and adapt. If we learned to survive with a job and something happened to that job and we are thrown into the wild of unemployment, this adaption feels much like the caged animal sent into the bush. When we are placed in circumstances where we have to take initiative and be creative, some of us find it hard.

If you have been trained to obey orders rather than think or have been unconsciously pledging allegiance to the average, you may have expected things to remain the same and feel ill-equipped when they don't. You may even forget that everything has a season and continue to operate as though it is winter while it is summer.

In times of high-pressure change, you will quickly discover that the old rules don't often apply and that you must adapt. You must become a quick study. It's not a matter of intelligence but of instinctive adaptability, which means you may not have the past training or experience to prepare you for these new challenges. But if you do not immediately recognize the vast changes in your environmental circumstances, then the opportunity for growth and innovative achievement closes.

You could be a leader and not know it. You could be a warm, loving person innately but not have had an opportunity to unpack what's inside of you. You could be an artist, a parent, a healer, a communicator and simply not have had the opportunity for adaptation yet.

Transitions are usually challenging. But while we often resist and feel unsettled, what is exciting is we are forced to discover new skill sets. Activating your faith will see you through change and help you learn to adapt. The fact that you may be experiencing trouble activating those internal instincts necessary for transition simply doesn't mean that you don't have it in you to do so. Realize that no matter how gifted you were at receiving income one way, it doesn't mean that you can't unearth the creativity and passion to receive it another way.

Remember that God is in control of all seasons of life. Knowing that God is with you through the changes can bring comfort and confidence. Just as the book of Matthew opens with the promise that Jesus will be "God with us" and closes with the words of Jesus: "I am with you always," we can be guaranteed that our God is with us throughout each changing moment. What a blessed assurance.

Remember the Creator of seasons when you face a season of change.

Prayer

Heavenly Lord, thank you for the reminder that you are in control of all situations and circumstances—even the changes I am learning to adapt to. Give me strength, wisdom, and courage to face new things with confidence and the assurance that you can lead and guide me in every place.

In Jesus' name. Amen.

78

REINVENT YOURSELF

Therefore, if anyone is in Christ, he is a new creation. The
old has passed away; behold, the new has come.
2 Corinthians 5:17, ESV

At some point in time, you will find yourself in between places, in between phases in life. This may be on a job where you've done all you can do, you've been as creative as you can be. This could be in a new season of life where someone has died or exited your life, leaving you facing an uncertain tomorrow. Perhaps your children have left home and you're wondering who you are. These are perfect times in life to reinvent yourself. It's the best time to look inside and find out who you are and who you've become. You can use your instincts to point the way for the next leg of your journey.

At this critical point in your life, you can reinvent yourself into the highest and best of who you were created to be. Tap into your core and assess what is there—hunger and thirst to follow your heart. You can decide to live from your center and flow in your gifts.

Your response and your attitude at this time in life will determine what comes out of you. You can bemoan what has passed, or you can call forth the thing that is inside of you to create a new path and a new life. You get the chance to break down what's inside of you and ask who you really are. You don't have to worry about what someone else wants you to be or who someone else thinks you should be. You have the opportunity to get to your core and decide: *I am going to be authentically who God has called me to be.*

God will give you the strength to birth again and build again. You will be able to move forward again—and you will no longer be captive to the place you are right now. You can benefit from all you've learned and all you've gone through.

Refuse to mope and romanticize what has left you—a job, a spouse, an opportunity. Assess the damage and jump back into the game with a renewed sense of who you are and all you have to offer to the world. Your instincts will be keener. Your intuition has been refined in the furnace of affliction. Live with robust excitement and enthusiasm. You are not dead. Make the most of whatever time you have left to live by truly living. God wants you to be fulfilled. Determine to live your life to the fullest.

❁ ❁ ❁ ❁

Prayer

I am a new creation. Each day that I awake, I have been given another chance to live this life to the fullest. I will take each and every lesson from this journey and use it to live authentically. I will live as you've designed me to live.

Amen.

79

STAY CENTERED

Remain in me, as I also remain in you. No branch can bear fruit by itself; it must remain in the vine. Neither can you bear fruit unless you remain in me.
John 15:4, NIV

So what do you do when you get attacked while following your instincts or entering new ventures with new partners? How do you survive and thrive in your destiny without becoming a blink in history? Once again, I learned from Bentley and Sable, my hairy, slobbering Roman Cane Corso friends. Their unique qualities have taught me to use who you are to adapt to where you find yourself and to not allow where you find yourself to make or define who you are.

As canines, they can't connect with the rabbits nor are they designed to. They can't climb trees with the squirrels or hide under roots like the chipmunks. They may resemble the coyote, but they aren't one of them. Perhaps that's why it's good that they have each other. The shared experience of frolicking like pets in the day and fighting like soldiers at night bonds them together.

They also share the love, attention, and sustenance offered by their owner. For, no matter what happens in the suburban of night—whether they return with birds in their mouths or blood on their torsos—they always come back to their home base. They know who they are, whose they are, and ultimately where they belong.

The same is true for you! Many people will want to use your mouth to convey their message. Don't let them. Others will try to harness your influence for their agenda. Resist them. There will be moments when someone steals your thunder, mauls your paws, and nips your nose. But you can always survive the treacheries and tragedies if you have a base to which you can return. Never allow the other animals to overwhelm you so much that you lose your way back to where you belong. Always know your base, that calm core of confidence within you, and how to access it and take shelter as needed.

As Christians, that base is Christ. We have to stay connected to our center, our anchor, our base. Run everything to the filter of God's Word, knowing you move and live and have your being in him (Acts 17:28). If it isn't like him, if it won't please him, don't do it. And that includes acting like someone you're not. If you believe you are following your God-given instincts, following the uniqueness of who you were created to be, be true to that. If you are connected to the vine, you need to stay connected—lest you stop being fruitful. You can't truly live out your purpose if you are not connected to your source, your vine, our Lord. Know your purpose and stay true to it.

You must be true to your purpose, doggedly tenacious about your passion, and never lose sight of your center. You can't be balanced without a center point upon which other forces tilt. That part that doesn't move within you controls all that is moving around you. If you lose your center and forgo your identity, then you're done, finished, kaput!

Whether you win or lose today's skirmish for survival doesn't matter as much as maintaining your base. I've seen my dogs come back to the house with possums in their mouths, wagging their tails with glee. I've also seen them come back with blood running down their legs with lacerations from a bobcat as their only reward. But they always come back to the base.

If you lose your sense of who you are, you have nothing to which you can return. If you don't discover your passions, purpose, and power, then you will pursue the roles assigned by other people's scripts. You will lose the success afforded by new opportunities if you don't know your own priorities and preferences.

Your strength is in your uniqueness. If you lose yourself just to get along with others, then you have nothing original to offer this new world of possibilities. In spy language, you have been compromised. In scientific language, you have been neutralized. In corporate language, you have become redundant. In short, you become liquidated, excommunicated, and eradicated!

Stay true to yourself while you integrate what you have into where you are. Chase the squirrels, fight the bobcats, and roll in the grass, but hold on to what makes you just as unique as my Roman Cane Corsos. Whether you're in victory or agony, you will always survive to fight another day if you refuse to compromise and make your instinctive calling your compass!

Prayer
Lord, I thank you for being my true vine and my connection to God's almighty power. Help me to always remain in you and true to who you created me to be—even when I'm tempted by other people and other things.
In Jesus' name. Amen.

BE WISE

God blesses everyone who has wisdom and common sense. Wisdom is worth more than silver; it makes you much richer than gold.

Proverbs 3:13-14, CEV

While it's wonderful to know what you know, wisdom requires that you also know what you don't know. There's much you already know. There's much more to be learned. And there's how what you know fits into what you do not know. This is what Solomon meant in Proverbs about finding wisdom and finding understanding. The two go hand in hand. Wisdom produces understanding. Intellect alone can't.

Prayer is always the start of wisdom. Tapping into your source and center will help you discern where you should be and how you should respond to the information flying at you from every direction. This instinct-following concept really is based in being connected to your compass and guide, your Creator, God.

I also caution you not to assume that you can rely on your instincts for information that's easily accessible in other ways. Gather the facts before you reflect on your feelings. Do your homework. Read what's necessary to be up to speed and well-informed about all angles of a problem, conflict, or issue. God makes these facts available; it's up to you to find them and use them.

Your instincts need to know the boundaries before they can help you get your bearings. Just as animals mark their territory so that they will recognize it later, we need to know the lay of the land before we begin traipsing through it. Without tending to the basics of investigation and research, it's impossible for our instincts to guide us accurately.

❁ ❁ ❁ ❁

Prayer
Wonderful Counselor, thank you for helping me to discern my boundaries, use the information presented to assess the situation, and pray for wisdom. I thank you for leading and guiding me.
In Jesus' name. Amen.

81

PRAYER IS POWERFUL

Very early the next morning, Jesus got up and went to a place where he could be alone and pray.
Mark 1:35, CEV

My prayer is not that you take them out of the world but that you protect them from the evil one. They are not of the world, even as I am not of it. Sanctify them by the truth; your word is truth.
John 17:15-17, NIV

Entering new territory and following your instinct can be exciting and invigorating. But don't forget to pack some essential tools, including your work ethic and ability to adapt to the new environment. And as you expand and explore new areas, make prayer the center of your life. It will keep you in tune with God and it will keep you in tune with your instincts.

Your new environment—whatever that might be—whether church, job, business, marriage, or partnership—needs to be studied carefully. You can do this by listening to your instincts as well as to your new associates. And remember, not all chemicals mix well! Chemical reactions can produce powerful results that either destroy or create energy for an organization. You want to gather the right mix to create powerful energy.

And while you can't go into a new environment and change everything on day one, you cannot be afraid to change when it is necessary. Learn to balance tradition and innovation. Record the habits of those in your new surroundings, but don't allow yourself to follow the same patterns unless you're making a deliberate choice.

Jesus, in his prayer for the disciples and believers, asked God to protect us from the evil in the world. He knew that we were still in the world, but we didn't have to be of the world. We didn't need to use the world's schemes to live fulfilled lives. We can follow Christ's example while he was here on earth. He mixed and mingled with many, but he didn't let them stop him from pursuing his purpose. He healed, taught, convicted, and became our ultimate sacrifice for sin. He didn't allow his environment to stop him from following what God put him on earth to do, but he still walked among the very people he was here to serve.

And you should follow Jesus' example—always. Don't succumb to the ways of the world, but don't fly so above the people that you are not able to relate to them or to meet their needs. Regardless of where you find yourself, you can still follow your purpose. Be aware of those in your new environment, but don't get caught up in their patterns if they do not match you or your purpose for being here.

Your presence changes the ecosystem and alters the environment for better and/or for worse. Your ability to survive has everything to do with your ability to remain true to your core.

Know your own proclivities and preferences, your default settings and disciplines. Protect your soft areas and use your strengths. Increasing the power of your instincts means learning more about yourself than ever before. Living a heart-felt life is fulfilling, yet requires intentionality and hard work.

Following your instincts into new territory is an especially important time to have a powerful prayer life. Jesus is our example. Scripture records that he got away often to pray. And even in today's Scripture—right before his journey to the cross—he is praying mightily and faithfully. Don't enter new territories without being prayed up—and staying prayed up. It can help you stand, true to your purpose and true to your God.

✿ ✿ ✿ ✿

Prayer
God in heaven who cares for the world, I commit myself to remain true to you and my purpose. Thank you for the awesome power of prayer which allows me to always call upon you. Draw me close to you as I enter new territory with new players.

In Jesus' name. Amen.

82

KNOW WHEN TO CHANGE

Pour new wine into new wineskins, and both are preserved.
Matthew 9:17b, NIV

Throughout this book, I've been very clear that change is inevitable and that true instinct followers learn to embrace it. But the big question remains: how do I retain what I need and release what I do not?

Your gifting and opportunity can bring you into a new arena that your skill sets may be able to manage but not maximize. With these new opportunities, your mentality is influenced not by where you're going but more aptly by where you've been. But surely you see the danger in such an approach. A new suit doesn't change the old man! A new hairdo won't transform the woman inside.

You can't function on the next level if you cling to the old you. Many people move into a new opportunity, but they have the past mentality; and soon they find that they are having experiences that poison the fresh chance with old contaminates. You can't live instinctively if you carry the methodology of where you were and not where you are! You can't communicate old messages, expound ideas that are passé, use language that is outdated, and repeat habits from the past. If you do, you are destined for self-sabotage! Tradition and innovation must work in harmony for maximum success, and our instincts know how to maintain this equilibrium.

Jesus is our Master Teacher, and we can learn from how he interacted with people even 2,000 years ago. Jesus followed some traditions—like going to the temple, being baptized, praying—but he surely also broke traditions to fit the need at the time. Whatever he did, it all pointed back to his purpose—to be about his father's business, to be true to his mission. So rules and regulations were not nearly as important as meeting needs when they all pointed back to his purpose.

In every way, we can seek to be more and more like Jesus every day, growing in wisdom and stature.

Meditate on what Jesus shared in Matthew 9 when John's disciples couldn't understand why Jesus' disciples weren't following the same rules that they were—or doing things like they were used to doing them. Jesus says: "No one sews a patch of unshrunk cloth on an old garment, for the patch will pull away from the garment, making the tear worse. Neither do people pour new wine into old wineskins. If they do, the skins will burst; the wine will run out and the wineskins will be ruined. No, they pour new wine into new wineskins, and both are preserved" (vv. 16-17). Just like clothing loosens with wear and tear, wine skins expand when the grapes ferment. If you pour new wine into an old wine skin, the skin would already be expanded and would break once the new wine started to ferment.

You use new with new. So during new times, you need to assess and decide what needs to be new—while not changing your core or your purpose, you can adapt to fit the present need.

Prayer
Dear Lord, teach me to always assess when I need to change my methods and adapt to the new.
In Jesus' name. Amen.

ONE SIZE DOES NOT FIT ALL

It's in Christ that we find out who we are and what we are living for. Long before we first heard of Christ and got our hopes up, he had his eye on us, had designs on us for glorious living, part of the overall purpose he is working out in everything and everyone.
Ephesians 1:11-12, MSG

God knew what he was doing from the very beginning. He decided from the outset to shape the lives of those who love him along the same lines as the life of his Son. The Son stands first in the line of humanity he restored. We see the original and intended shape of our lives there in him. After God made that decision of what his children should be like, he followed it up by calling people by name. After he called them by name, he set them on a solid basis with himself. And then, after getting them established, he stayed with them to the end, gloriously completing what he had begun.
Romans 8:29-30, MSG

When you operate based on a formula of one-size-fits-all, you miss the power and insight that your instincts can bring. It's similar to trying to follow the exact path of someone else to receive their success. The operative word here is "their." It is what they have been called to do with what God has deposited inside of them. And while your calling can be similar, your experiences, your inner wiring, your makeup, your perspective, your world view, your culture, and so on are fundamentally different.

When you begin to understand instinct, you begin to understand that only you can do what God has called—predestined—you to do. And only you should do it with your specific set of skills, experiences, flair, and instinct. God had a plan when he created each of us. God shaped us to fulfill a mission—just as Christ fulfilled the ultimate mission.

So you will now have more reason to invest the time and energy, the hard work and personal evaluation to find out what you are created for. You will peel back the surface, the outward appearances, and look to your core to find out who you are and what you have to contribute in your own special way.

We do ourselves a disservice when we don't spend the needed resources to find our core. We have not been trained to do this, and we often short-change ourselves and others. Birds know that they should fly; they instinctively know this and with just a little push from Mama

Bird, they leave their nests and soar.

We need to learn to live by instinct, to follow our inner voice that tells us which way to go and what we should be doing. It is instinctive. We need to tap into it and follow it. Great fulfillment awaits all who do. You've been shaped for this.

Prayer
Amazing God, you have shaped and formed me for a specific calling and mission. I desire to know exactly what I should do and how I should do it. Because you designed me, you can reveal my core to me. I look to you and your plan for my life so that I can live fully and fulfilled. I thank you.
Amen.

WHEN CONFLICT ARISES

Blessed are the merciful: for they shall obtain mercy. Blessed are the pure in heart: for they shall see God. Blessed are the peacemakers: for they shall be called the children of God.
Matthew 5:7-9, KJV

Leading by instinct can become contagious. The people you influence—whether in business or in the home—will likely respond to your energy, example, and effort. Reward them by remaining relevant and supplying them with opportunities to stay cutting edge.

Leaders and followers have to be vigilant to maintain progress and innovation. Just because people stay married doesn't mean that they are happily married. Just because you've been with a company a long time doesn't mean that you have remained valuable.

You've got to grow forward and not just go forward. Growth is compromised when vitality dissipates and if the stagnancy sets in.

Whenever "what was" competes against "what is," the future —what can be—is jeopardized! So pay attention to those you lead—the pack. You don't want trouble seeping in and rising through your ranks. It can start off small but impact a full batch, like yeast (Galatians 5:9). The pack follows you—your energy, example, and effort. Be sure you address troubling issues quickly. If something is wrong, don't wait. Don't ignore it. Call it out. Don't let discontent rise within the pack. Confusion and discord can become contagious and spread. That's not what you want to spread; you want following instincts to become contagious!

A good model to follow is found in Jesus' teachings known as the Beatitudes (Matthew 5:1-12). It's in this passage that Jesus teaches how we should treat others. He is clear that those who show mercy will be shown the same. And he says the pure-hearted will see God. He also exhorts the peacemaker and says they will be called children of God. Jesus is saying that true followers of Christ are peacemakers. They look to establish peace whenever and wherever they can—and quickly. Being a peacemaker doesn't mean avoiding conflict; in fact, peacemakers look for conflict and address it with wisdom so they can bring resolution and peace quickly.

Examine your leadership style today. Look for ways you can bring more peace into situations—quickly.

✪ ✪ ✪ ✪

Prayer

Omniscient Lord, I will lead by my instincts. Give me wisdom to know how to handle problems before they spread and affect others. I seek to follow where you lead. I seek to bring peace quickly when conflict arises. I want to be called a child of God.

In Jesus' name. Amen.

85

BUILDERS AND BANKERS

As Jesus and his disciples were on their way, he came to a
village where a woman named Martha opened her home to
him. She had a sister called Mary, who sat at the Lord's feet
listening to what he said. But Martha was distracted by all
the preparations that had to be made. She came to him and
asked, "Lord, don't you care that my sister has left me to do
the work by myself? Tell her to help me!"
Luke 10:38-40, NIV

Here a dinner was given in Jesus' honor. Martha
served, while Lazarus was among those reclining at the table
with him. Then Mary took about a pint of pure nard, an
expensive perfume; she poured it on Jesus' feet and wiped
his feet with her hair. And the house was filled with the
fragrance of the perfume.
John 12:2-3, NIV

We are all leaders in some way, and we can act like
bankers or builders. Instinct-led leaders know both are
required for healthy growth and advancement.

Builders are motivated by challenge. They have to have something to build, fight, or that gives them quantifiable results. They keep the atmosphere vibrant and can be spontaneous, are always creative, and engage most when there is action.

Bankers are like wood-burning stoves. They feel a sense of achievement from maintenance. They are great at putting into place critical systems to make sure that everything operates well. They tend to be consistent, methodical, and most engaged when things are sedate.

Builders make money; bankers save it. Builders keep the marriage exciting; bankers keep the home grounded. Builders can draw a crowd; bankers can train the crowd that gathers.

Both are required for the growth of a healthy company, relationship, or endeavor. The dynamic, productive tension between them works beautifully until you put a banker in charge of project development or a new business acquisition, or put the builder in charge of the bottom line projections and detailed maintenance! The banker values what is. The builder values fresh incentives and unrealized opportunity. All groups need builders and bankers. All instinctive leaders recognize which is their strongest tendency.

Once you recognize your builder or banker instinct, it's about having the right people in your life and also about having the right mix.

Consider Mary and Martha, the friends of Jesus. Martha was a builder, very active and busy producing the meal and making sure her guests, particularly Jesus, were cared for. She was best when in action. Mary was a banker—much happier sitting at the feet of Jesus, listening and learning from him, anointing his feet with expensive perfume. Martha wanted Mary to get up and help her—to be a builder like her—and she asked Jesus to correct Mary. But Jesus understood that both women were needed to make guests feel welcomed—someone needed to keep company, someone needed to serve. Jesus' words that Mary had chosen the right thing, doesn't obscure the fact that together these two women—a builder and a banker—created a hospitable place for their guests. They were both very much needed.

In my organization, we've worked hard to create the needed balance between bankers and builders. As you explore all your leadership opportunities—not just the ones at the office—make sure you use instinct to understand whether you are a builder or a banker and to make sure you have the right mix of people on your team.

❁ ❁ ❁ ❁

Prayer

Almighty Lord, I thank you for reminding me to have balance—in my life and in my work. I know that both builders and bankers are needed to do the work you've called me to. I desire to honor and empower both the Marys and Marthas in my life.

In Jesus' name. Amen.

SUPPORT SYSTEMS

Moses' father-in-law [Jethro] replied, "What you are doing is not good. You and these people who come to you will only wear yourselves out. The work is too heavy for you; you cannot handle it alone. Listen now to me and I will give you some advice, and may God be with you. You must be the people's representative before God and bring their disputes to him. Teach them his decrees and instructions, and show them the way they are to live and how they are to behave. But select capable men from all the people—men who fear God, trustworthy men who hate dishonest gain—and appoint them as officials over thousands, hundreds, fifties and tens. Have them serve as judges for the people at all times, but have them bring every difficult case to you; the simple cases they can decide themselves. That will make your load lighter, because they will share it with you. If you do this and God so commands, you will be able to stand the strain, and all these people will go home satisfied."

Exodus 18:17-23, NIV

As you learn to rely on your instinct and see your territory expand, there is an important lesson to learn about building a team and using your support system. While it is sometimes tempting to be a lone ranger and an independent person, the wise leader understands the significance of a solid support system. And not only does wisdom know about a support system, wisdom uses that support system effectively.

If you rely only on yourself, you are limited; you are your only resource. Independent leaders may be surrounded by people but refuse to rely on others. In fact, people typically don't assist independent leaders because they look like they can handle it all alone. If you send the signal that you don't need help, then others will receive it accordingly.

While I applaud that you can do it alone, always remember that if you can do a task, you will always have a job. But if you know why the task must be tackled, then you can delegate it to others to work for or with you!

Even Moses needed to learn this lesson; and his father-in-law, Jethro was a wise counselor. When he saw how much Moses was doing, he advised him to get help. He advised Moses to focus on the big picture of what God had called him to do—teach the people God's laws and bring their cries to God—but to seek help for the other tasks. Keep in mind all of the tasks were connected to Moses' purpose, but he wasn't the only one who could handle every task. Jethro told Moses this would prevent him from burning out and would satisfy the people.

There's a way to get it done; you don't have to be the only one to do it all!

✪ ✪ ✪ ✪

Prayer
Loving Lord, I know I need to balance my independence
with my need for help. Remind me that I'm not an island
and to effectively develop and use my support system.
In Jesus' name. Amen.

INSPIRE OTHERS

Moses listened to his father-in-law and did everything he said. He chose capable men from all Israel and made them leaders of the people, officials over thousands, hundreds, fifties and tens. They served as judges for the people at all times. The difficult cases they brought to Moses, but the simple ones they decided themselves.
Exodus 18:24-26, NIV

To lead by your instincts is to inspire those around you. Leading by instinct requires you to influence others and amass support. If you are to achieve the dreams set before you, it will require support—a team effort. Your instincts can help you assemble the best team and influence them. Knowing what motivates those around you to new heights is part of this instinctive influence. Managing conflict, creating innovative solutions, and maintaining your strength of character and moral center also influence others.

People instinctively want to trust the leader they follow. They want to believe that he or she is worthy of their investment of time and effort. They want to know that their leaders will recognize their value and enhance their skill set. Instinctive leaders know that if they cannot engage those around them, their boundaries shrink.

Another reason to include and empower others is that when you operate independently in the midst of your team, it stunts their growth as well as your own. If you want to lead by your instincts, then you must create a vision large enough that you cannot achieve it alone. You want something so much bigger than you that you must delegate to a team.

Interdependence is the real indicator that a strong leader is emerging. Anything you can lead alone isn't much. You want something that is so far beyond your own capabilities that it will require a task force to achieve the goal. So don't pick something your own size. Make your dreams big enough for your team to grow into them.

If you have the courage to take on a project that requires assistance, other gifted people will become invested in your cause. I've found that people are much more willing to galvanize around a mission and not just a man. Inspirational leaders ignite a spark within us that compels us to be part of the blaze that they are lighting. When you inspire people to come on board with you, you are evolving into an instinctive leader. Instinctive leadership will not only get you great results, it will empower others to follow their instincts too. Imagine the power in a team all following their instincts.

✿ ✿ ✿ ✿

Prayer
Holy One, I am thankful for my support system. I will lead them by instinct and by example. Show me how to inspire each team member to be their best and to follow their God-given instincts.
In Jesus' name.

88

LEAD UNDER FIRE

*I have told you these things, so that in me you may have
peace. In this world you will have trouble. But take heart! I
have overcome the world.*

John 16:33, NIV

*The LORD is my light and my salvation; Whom shall I fear?
The LORD is the strength of my life; Of whom shall I be
afraid?*

Psalm 27:1, NKJV

I can tell a lot about an instinctive leader by the way he
or she responds to troublesome dilemmas. Life will
bring challenges; that's biblical. Jesus said: "In this
world, you will have trouble"! Try all you want to avoid
trouble, but you're liable to run into a tornado when running away from a windstorm! Sometimes you can know all
that research can teach you and will have memorized all
kinds of contingency plans; and yet when trouble strikes,
you discover fears you didn't know you had.

I once employed a security agent who knew volumes of information about law enforcement, protection, and crime prevention. He could teach the role, and he definitely looked the part. However, his intellect could not compensate for weak instincts. When we encountered gunplay at the Dallas-Fort Worth airport, he actually ran off and left me in the middle of the danger!

My security agent was not a bad person, but he simply could not be effective in a reactive situation. He could talk about hypothetical scenarios and classroom defense techniques, but in the heat of real danger, his training went out the window. Needless to say, I replaced him with someone whose knowledge was matched by their instinctive leadership.

Under pressure, we have a tendency to go to our default settings. I guess his default instinct was stuck on flight instead of fight. Maybe you or I would've been tempted to do the same in a similar situation; it's fascinating to see what pressure produces in any of us. Sometimes we can't know our instincts from our insecurities until we go from the frying pan into the fire a few times.

While most of us are not placed in life-threatening situations, we do face turmoil that threatens our family, our company, or our income. Whatever the threat, we all face fears every day. When effective leaders are stressed or fearful, they have to rely on their instincts to survive. When the wind blows, whether gentle breeze or bitter blast, you must stand strong.

The better you are at responding to a challenge, the more apt you are to succeed.

Instinctive leaders set the trend. They respond to crises and handle the mishaps of life, minimizing damages and maximizing opportunities. An instinctive leader radiates an air of confidence and composure that attracts and energizes those around them.

Instinctive leaders manage the dismal, the distracted, and the dangerous. They view these impositions and oppositions as opportunities to test their strength, exercise their talent, and expand their vision. It is stressful but rewarding, tiring yet tempting. Instinctive leadership finds accomplishment in its ability to navigate a response to challenges by proactive and reactive reasoning. They live by Psalm 27: "The Lord is my strength, whom shall I fear?" When instinctive leaders' trust and power are connected to God's resurrection power (Ephesians 1:19), stormy conditions will not stop them. Instead, they dig in, plant their feet firmly, and activate their instincts.

Prayer

Almighty and powerful God, I know that trouble is just a part of life, but you are with me every step of the way. I trust you to help me to stand strong when the winds of life blow.

Amen.

89

FLEX AND STRETCH

For those who exalt themselves will be humbled, and those who humble themselves will be exalted.
Luke 14:11, NLT

In order to establish balance between intellect and instinct, you need agility and flexibility. Like a tightrope walker tilting one way and then another, compensating here and readjusting there, you must stay loose and responsive. The power of instinct-driven success relies on your ability to adjust and adapt. Instinctive leadership relies on this same dexterity.

Instinctive flexibility requires what I call "360-degree thinking." Being flexible includes the understanding that anything you do affects everyone connected to you. Think in a panoramic way of all who will be affected by each move you make. Understand that you have no right to expect those around you to comply with a vision you haven't shared and expectations you haven't articulated.

Process all variables instinctively before making any final decision. Think through the options, possibilities, and contingencies. Remain flexible enough to make adjustments when needed. Always assess where you are. Think again of the tightrope walker who is constantly gauging where his foot has landed. Will his next step need to be different? Will she need to extend her hands further to gain balance? Does she need to tune out more noise so she can focus and know just where to place her next step?

Make sure you have a strategy that anticipates all the variables, rather than only focusing on your own accomplishment. At the heart of flexibility is humility. The leader who considers others needs before their own is truly humble—and Christ-like. This type of leader in the end will be exalted and successful.

The 360 concept works because you consider the effects of your goal or actions on everyone affected by it. Go full circle and look at your new endeavor from all angles. Not considering everything is the equivalent of not considering anything. Until you have implemented 360-degree thinking, you aren't prepared for the increase that comes from following your instincts. You may have a great backup plan that manages crises but you may not have a strategy for success. If you don't think in a circle, you will leave some area unprotected. Wherever planning ends, problems begin!

Write down the areas where you lead others and draw a circle around each one. Then write down the name of every person, place, or thing your leadership affects. You may be shocked by how many individuals you affect. You wouldn't want inflexibility to stunt your growth and impact. Be flexible and carefully place your foot on the tightrope. You can hold your balance.

✿ ✿ ✿ ✿

Prayer

Amazing and merciful God, teach me to remain flexible when considering the needs of others. I desire to follow the example of Christ and to consider others' needs even as I consider my own needs. I ask you to be with each person I interact with this day. Show me how to inspire them.

In Jesus' name. Amen.

90

IT'S ALL FOR A REASON

We know that God is always at work for the good of every-one who loves him. They are the ones God has chosen for his purpose.

Romans 8:28, CEV

Listening to your instincts gives you one of the best chances to make a real and meaningful difference in the world around you.

The ground you walk upon reverberates with the decisions you make and echoes with your lifestyle choices. Instinctive influence cannot be contrived, controlled, or regulated. With your instincts come collaboration and co-operation. Once you have a sense of living by instinct, you will connect people, places, and things in a way you never imagined.

Before long, your simultaneous environments will align like spokes in a wheel that has you as its hub. And as your circle of contact continues to enlarge, you will be able to cover more ground with each revolution.

But this is not about turning the wheel faster or winning a race; it's about your direction, your purpose. Connectivity must not be used to inflame the greedy or empower the selfish. It provides a guide to unearthing your power to function in various orbits for a purpose greater than yourself. It is this pursuit that lands you in a broader context, exploring new possibilities and challenging limitations. Fulfilling your own destiny allows others to fulfill theirs.

In essence, your influence is about others; it's about serving; it is about the letting God be in charge. Your operating by your God-given instincts will impact other people regardless of what it is you're doing. God creates these types of interactions, for everything was created for God and by God (Colossians 1:16). Your very life will work together for the good of others, which brings God glory and blesses you. If you're following instincts, your purpose will point back to your Creator and will bless God's people.

Prayer
Creator of the world, you have created me for a purpose
and I desire to follow your plans for my life. Use my gifts
and mission to impact others in all I do and say so that
your people may be blessed and you will get the glory
and honor.
In Jesus' name. Amen.

91

DREAM AND DISCOVER

Now to him who is able to do immeasurably more than all we ask or imagine, according to his power that is at work within us, to him be glory in the church and in Christ Jesus throughout all generations, for ever and ever! Amen.
Ephesians 3:20-21, NIV

Where are your instincts leading you? Although you never know where your instinctive gifts may lead, this doesn't mean that you don't set your GPS on a destination! Look around the corner and consider where you want to be in six months, two years, a decade from now. Allow yourself to dream; you could find something you didn't anticipate. And at the very least, you know which way to point your feet.

You can never begin this process too early. Freedom is often as much a state of mind as it is a state of being. The amazing power of God to do more than we think and imagine enlarges our dreams. So expand your thoughts;

roam around and get some ideas. You never know what God could be up to and where your instincts could lead you. Your imagination is not the limit!

Don't let your lack of resources—or lack of time and energy—stop you. If God has brought it to your vision, it is possible. If it is a part of God's plan, God will help you find a way to make it happen. Oftentimes, what you need is to take a first step. Then more and more resources will become available to you. So instead of wondering how in the world you can make this happen, ask yourself one or two things you need to get started. Find those things, and remain flexible enough to find those things in unexpected places. Are there classes you can take? Apprenticeships you can sign up for? Workshops? Conferences? Do a little bit, and watch God do more.

✪ ✪ ✪ ✪

Prayer
Awesome and powerful God, I am fully aware that you are able to do more than I can even think or imagine. Take the blinders off of my imaginations and take the conditions off of my dreams. Show me the first step to take and give me the faith and courage to follow. I know you will open many doors for me to fulfill what you have called me to do.
Amen.

92

BOTH, AND

You prepare a table before me in the presence of my enemies.
You anoint my head with oil; my cup overflows. Surely your
goodness and love will follow me all the days of my life, and
I will dwell in the house of the LORD forever.
Psalm 23:5-6, NIV

As we learn to live instinctively, we often mistakenly think we must eliminate or compromise one opportunity for another. But here's the news flash: this isn't either-or! It's both, and.

Many times people choose "what's next" at the expense of "what is now." You could start a business *and* keep your career. You could explore your passion for music *and* start a family. You could remain on the corporate ladder *and* pursue completing your college degree. Not either-or but both, and. It is possible to add without subtracting.

The idea of managing more intimidates some people because they add by subtracting. Their way is to add this, take away that, and basically trade one for the other. They forget about creative, strategic moves that adapt to both, and.

Your cup is supposed to run over. It's not just what David sang to the Lord in the 23rd Psalm. It's what we proclaim, too. God can make your cup run over—both, and. Your cup not only overflows with abundance in your own life, but into the lives of those around you. Your ability to handle multiple opportunities directly affects your family, workplace, church, and community.

Most highly successful and accomplished people have mastered many worlds. Look to such people in your life as role models, mentors, and teachers; and it will change the way you perceive choices, even obstacles on your path. You can be both philanthropic *and* profitable; you can work *and* volunteer, raise children *and* have a career, if you catch the principle of both, and—the principle of your cup running over.

You will add to what you have without losing what you've accomplished if you stop holding everything so tightly and learn to juggle and let God make your cup run over!

❂ ❂ ❂ ❂

Prayer
Lord, I thank you for the revelation to live with my expectations increased. Help me to see new responsibilities as opportunities to bless your people as my cup overflows. I thank you for I am truly grateful.

In Jesus' name. Amen.

93

HEART WORK

Come near to God and he will come near to you.
James 4:8a, NIV

Have you ever seen someone have a heart attack? Their eyes go dim, their pulse stops, their mouth goes dry, and their pupils dilate. Why do such reactions happen in the head when it's the heart that's malfunctioning? Obviously, the head along with the rest of the body manifest the effects of the heart shutting down. It is from the heart that the head and body have life.

What's stored deeply within your heart? If the answer eludes you, you may need more time for inner work. The best way to discover what is in your heart is to seek and to continuously grow close to God.

James tells us how to get pure hearts. We must remember that God is always near; we are the ones who need to draw close to our Creator. Someone once said that if you don't feel close to God, ask yourself who did the moving. As we draw closer to God through prayer, reading and meditating upon Scripture, worshiping, and fellowshipping with believers, we will surely feel more of God's presence. God hasn't moved or left us; we just have to draw closer.

James instructs us to submit ourselves to God and resist the devil (v. 7). He further exhorts us to get rid of anything that isn't pure, anything that is not like God, anything that separates us from God (v. 8b). By submitting fully to God, we discover what's in our hearts. "Cleanse your heart" means to examine your motivations and feelings and work on ridding yourself of any that are not pleasing to God and loving toward others. Through that cleansing process, you become pure and boldly ready to pursue all God has for you.

Commit to seeking God fully today. Commit to purifying your heart today. Commit to uncovering the inner desires and passions God has implanted in your heart. What's in your heart is the key to meaning in your life.

Prayer
Holy God who is so near me, as I examine my motivations and feelings, I know there are many that are not pleasing to you and not loving toward others. I place them honestly before you. I trust that you are, in this moment, replacing them with right thinking and right behavior and that, bit by bit, my heart will be pure before you.
In Jesus' name. Amen.

94

THE PRIZE

Pay careful attention to your own work, for then you will get the satisfaction of a job well done, and you won't need to compare yourself to anyone else.
Galatians 6:4; NLT

In all thy ways acknowledge [God], and he shall direct thy paths.
Proverbs 3:6, KJV

I press toward the mark for the prize of the high calling of God in Christ Jesus.
Philippians 3:14, KJV

If you have ever had the privilege of knowing an instinct follower, you know this person can take the mundane and make it magical. They can take simple equipment and produce superlative results. Often they maximize their general training with their unique flair.

They have that extra something that others don't seem to have or don't tap into.

Fulfilling one's true potential is not about doing what other people expect, or the appearance of winning rather than committing to the practices and hard work that create a true champion. The prize is not the art of winning. Some will ultimately buy a trophy without ever running a race. They didn't take the class; they bought the diploma. They aren't successful; they just have the props. They aren't driven to achieve; they just appear busy to everyone around them.

The irony that these people fail to realize is: when you're living by instinct, you will naturally enhance everything and everyone around you. In other words, success will come naturally! When both your intellect and instincts are aligned, the fruit of your labor brings satisfaction beyond measure.

It will still require hard work and dedication, but the internal satisfaction will fuel your desire to achieve even larger dreams. When you don't become fixated on winning the prize or appearing successful and instead pursue your passions, you will discover the fulfillment that comes from living by instinct.

Solomon says we can do nothing better than to find satisfaction—fulfillment—in our work. We are put here for a short time—and none of us know how long we have to live. But a life well-lived is one that comes from living out our divine destiny, our reason for being here.

Acknowledging God as Creator and the giver of your purpose puts you in line to follow God's will. It sets the stage for you to discover your passions and to work in harmony with them. This is where you will find satisfaction.

✿ ✿ ✿ ✿

Prayer
Lord, I want to be fulfilled and to do your will. I know that is the prize of life. I affirm that the way I live and the work I put into accomplishments is what brings honor and glory to you.
In Jesus' name. Amen.

95

FORMAL AND INFORMAL EDUCATION

For nothing is impossible with God.
                    Luke 1:37, NLT

Your promises have been thoroughly tested, and your servant loves them.
                    Psalm 119:140, NIV

Not everyone has had the opportunity to receive degrees. Some of us were limited by finances, exposure, or other life circumstances. But don't become discouraged by that fact. Your life can have purpose without formal education.

Men and women who are quite intelligent and successful, often didn't earn a degree. An instinctive decision or instinctive move was the key to their success. They had great instincts and were dialed into them and acted on them. These men and women listened to the promptings within them and had the courage to derail the scripted plans of their lives and, by inner impulse, chart their courses.

They listened to that nebulous space in the human soul that houses a personal navigational system—one that all of us have, even if in most of us it's often underutilized. This innate compass provides guidance in answering the age-old questions: Why am I here? What can I do with the life, gifts, and opportunities I have been allotted?

So, my friend, while education is important, it is also just as important to remember that it can be obtained formally and informally. Pursuing your passions and following instinct is much more about tapping into your inner navigational system and pulling out your best. It's having faith to act upon those ideas nested inside of you and seizing the moment to activate your instinct.

Prayer
You, O God, are amazing and awesome. You fulfill your promises to me. I believe that you will provide all you have said, and I thank you for choosing me in all of my humanness to fulfill this mission.

96

NO AGE LIMIT

I will pour out my Spirit on all people. Your sons and daughters will prophesy, your old men will dream dreams, your young men will see visions.
Joel 2:28, NIV

We can learn a great deal by observing true instinct followers. They are innovators, and they live by their instincts to break barriers and resist complacency. When we look at these individuals, it's not enough to simply applaud their success; we must examine what they did and learn why they did it like they did it.

But the real catalyst of creative instincts is about peeking into the windows of your own heart and soul. Others can inspire you, but ultimately the only thing that empowers you is what lies within you and learning how to better utilize what you've been given. And there's never a better time to learn this than now. You are not too young and you can definitely never be too old to decide to tap into your instinct and follow your mission.

Even if what you've been given seems wrapped in nothing but problems, these barriers can become breakthroughs. They are blessings camouflaged as burdens. Problems develop endurance, which leads to character development, strength, and hope (Romans 5:3-4, NLT)—some good stuff. Whether you are wrestling with a poor marriage, a pathetic career, or a plummeting business, any area of your life can be transformed by your instincts if you're willing to look within and exercise them.

Go beyond the facts and failures, and explore the feelings and impulses you have to increase what you've been given. You will light a trailblazing torch that will illuminate your steps, spark your dreams, and nourish your aspirations.

I often tell people that the second part of their life should be better than the first part. Why? Because you've learned so much from the mistakes you've made and the mishaps you've had; a true instinct follower will activate those lessons and live empowered. They are now students of their gifts and inclinations and are not afraid to use them. And when God's Spirit comes upon you, you can dream dreams and see visions—at any age. You can fulfill your God-given mission.

There's no time like the present to start following your instincts and to use everything that has happened to you to propel you forward!

✪ ✪ ✪ ✪

Prayer

Gracious and Holy God, I come asking you to help me dream again. I desire to see the vision you have for my life and to follow it. You are an awesome God, and I ask that you pour your Spirit on me so that I might know how to follow my inner drive.

Amen.

97

KNOW HOPE

*I pray also that the eyes of your heart may be enlightened
in order that you may know the hope to which he has called
you, the riches of his glorious inheritance in his holy people.*
Ephesians 1:18, NIV

In this passage in Ephesians, Paul is basically telling the
church that he is praying that God will open their eyes
so they will know why they were called, so they will
know their purpose.

Look at the words closely. Paul wants the Christians to
be enlightened, to know more, to understand. And where
is this understanding coming from? It's not from the head;
it's not from text books; it's not from other people. It is
from the heart. Paul wants God to open the eyes of our
heart—this is where our instinct lies. This is the center of
our emotions and motivations. This is where those deep
desires and inclinations have been placed—right there in
our hearts.

And when our eyes are opened to our heart and we understand that God has called us to hope, then we are ready to start living instinctively.

Once your eyes open and you are inclined to hear what's in your heart, you can view your circumstances differently. You understand your trials as lessons for the future. You embrace challenges and rough times as places where you developed. You recognize darkness as a time of focusing and gearing up for the light. You realize that where you are is an incubator. It's not your destination; it is transportation. Where you are now can take you to the place you were destined and designed to be. Your heart is open and ready to receive your hope.

Instinctive living is at the core heart-felt living. Know that God has a plan for your life; it's up to you to activate all your Creator has already deposited in you so that you can press on to your mark—a high calling.

Prayer
Holy and merciful God, open my heart so that I may see
all you have deposited in me. Open my eyes so that I may
see circumstances through your eyes with faith that all
things are possible.
Amen.

98

FOR SUCH A TIME AS THIS

And who knows but that you have come to your royal position for such a time as this?
Esther 4:14b, NIV

The story of Queen Esther can give us great inspiration when we consider activating our instincts and living a more focused, mission-minded life. Esther was not born into a royal, prestigious family; in fact, she was an orphan. Her parents had died and her relative Mordecai, who speaks the critical words in today's passage, raises her. When King Xerxes calls for a new queen, Esther enters the so-called beauty contest. By preparing for almost a year and gaining wisdom from counselors, she is groomed for a royal position and is selected as the next queen.

But Esther isn't just royalty. She is connected to her heritage. She could stay in the palace and ignore what's going on—a planned attack on her people. She could turn a blind eye to the plight she has come from; she is after all in the palace now. But, as Mordecai tells her: "Perhaps you were chosen as Queen, placed in a position of authority and influence for such a time as this." Mordecai is reminding her that her job as a queen isn't only to look pretty and serve the king. She can use her position to help her people. And perhaps this is why God has brought her to this place at this time.

If you read the entire book of Esther, you'll find that Esther does risk her life and her position and approaches the king to intervene for her people. She uses wisdom as well as her influence to help others.

What about you? Reflect on your life's journey. What places has God allowed you to enter—whether palaces or prisons, the ghetto or the country club? Meditate on how your location in life—past and present—can be used at this time to help God's people. Decide today that you will use your unique journey to influence how you follow your instincts and live out your calling. God doesn't make mistakes. Nothing is happenstance. Use the events of your life—this great up and down roller coaster of a ride called life—to impact the environment around you.

You've been called. You've been prepared. Only you can do what God has deposited inside of you. Now is the time, and you have been designed for such a time as this.

❂ ❂ ❂ ❂

Prayer
Almighty God, I know that nothing is happenstance.
You have allowed me to walk this path on my journey
for a reason. I desire to use what you've deposited in me
to impact those around me. Thank you for creating me
for such a time as this. I will seize the moment and act
accordingly.
Amen.

99

GET YOUR MIND RIGHT

Do not conform to the pattern of this world, but be transformed by the renewing of your mind. Then you will be able to test and approve what God's will is—his good, pleasing and perfect will.

Romans 12:2, NIV

Instincts follow what's buried deep inside of your heart; but your head, or mind, plays a large role in your instincts too. You have to work on getting your mind right if you really want to live instinctively.

Scripture reminds us to renew our mind. The mind is powerful. Everything starts in your mind. It's your core. When you decide to do something, it must begin in your mind—and the same holds true for living by instinct.

You've got to transform your mind to live instinctively. Transforming your mind means looking inside of you to know what works for you—in essence, what turns you on. Transformation starts by identifying your core.

At the core of fruit is its seed, and the fruit can only become the kind of fruit that seed at its core produces. Tomatoes don't come from an apple. You can only be transformed into what you were created to be. And you can take the seed that is your core—your passions, proclivities, and giftings—and turn it into the highest form possible. Think tomato tree, tomato drink, a great tomato salad. But you've got to work with what you have. Renew your mind to know God's will. Prove what God had in mind when he made you so you can shine at what you were created to be.

When you transform your mind, you will be able to know what God's will is—what it is for you. What you were created and designed to do. And this all goes back to your core, your purpose, your central station.

Put effort into your core—what's central to you. Know yourself. Get to know yourself, what you need and want.

Never look at the peelings; look at the core. Know who you are so you can know what fits your core. Don't pick people or jobs or partners by the peelings—because you never get down to the core. Instead you could end up with something that looks appealing on the outside, but really it is not compatible with your core. Your purpose is contained in your core. And it's knowing your core that helps you find prosperity and true fulfillment.

Many people spend lots of time in places that are not central to their core. They've looked at the peelings—the things that appeal aesthetically, not the things that appeal to who they are inside. Transforming your mind will reveal who you are at the core, show what you do right, and determine the way you look at jobs, people, and your purpose.

If you transform your mind, you will know what God has designed you for. Renew your mind and find God's will for your life.

Prayer
God, I am transformed by the renewing of my mind.
Reveal to me what you have planted inside of me so I
will be better able to live instinctively. I desire to chase
my passion so I can be the highest form of who you have
created me to be.
In Jesus' name. Amen.

100

YOUR STRENGTH

But those who hope in the Lord will renew their strength.
They will soar on wings like eagles; they will run and not
grow weary, they will walk and not be faint.
Isaiah 40:31, NIV

Instincts allow your internal vision to become an external reality. Often this process of actualization may involve unexpected and even unorthodox methods of discovery and application. The art of being a visionary is to make the inside vision materialize outside.

Your instincts not only give voice to your innovative visions, but they transform mistakes into a mosaic masterpiece. They help you show outwardly what God has already manifested in you internally.

Often we look to others for inspiration, approval, or affirmation; but you, my friend, are the singular, most effective source for outwardly manifesting all the visions that are part of your gifting.

If you produce outwardly what you possess inwardly, many may imitate what you do; but none can duplicate what you do. If you follow your instincts from the inside out, you emerge in a class all by yourself. There is no one quite like you!

You were created to bring something to this earth that has never crystallized throughout the eons of time. You may not have fully discovered it yet; but if you live and lead by your instincts, your rare, precious, and one-of-a-kind gift will emerge!

Don't worry about where you will get your resources—money, energy, strength. Put your faith and hope and trust in God, the supplier of all your needs. God's Word promises to renew your strength. You can soar like an eagle and run this race without giving out. Your strength comes from the Lord. Tap into the power available to you. Live by your instincts and unleash all that God has planted inside of you. Fly, eagle, fly!

❂ ❂ ❂ ❂

Prayer
My Strength and my Provider, I know you have promised to renew my strength and provide all of my needs. I rely on you, with faith and hope, to supply what I need to run this race. I desire to soar and live out my life's mission so that I may help others and glorify you. I am ready to run and not faint. Unleash my inner drive so I can fly to new heights.
In Jesus' name. Amen.